高等学校试用教材

建筑类专业英语
建筑管理与财会

第一册

陆铁镛	孙 玮	主编
文育玲 李 红 吴来安		编
黄 莉 唐之远 彭志军		
任 宏		主审

中国建筑工业出版社

《建筑类专业英语》编审委员会

总 主 编　徐铁城
总 主 审　杨匡汉
副总主编　（以姓氏笔画为序）
　　　　　王庆昌　乔梦铎　陆铁镛
　　　　　周保强　蔡英俊
编　　委　（以姓氏笔画为序）
　　　　　王久愉　王学玲　王翰邦　卢世伟
　　　　　孙　玮　李明章　朱满才　向小林
　　　　　向　阳　刘文瑛　余曼筠　孟祥杰
　　　　　张少凡　张文洁　张新建　赵三元
　　　　　阎岫峰　傅兴海　褚羞花　蔡慧俭
　　　　　濮宏魁
责任编辑　庞大中

前　言

　　经过几十年的探索，外语教学界许多人认为，工科院校外语教学的主要目的，应该是："使学生能够利用外语这个工具，通过阅读去获取国外的与本专业有关的科技信息。"这既是我们建设有中国特色的社会主义的客观需要，也是在当前条件下工科院校外语教学可能完成的最高目标。事实上，教学大纲规定要使学生具有"较强"的阅读能力，而对其他方面的能力只有"一般"要求，就是这个意思。

　　大学本科的一、二年级，为外语教学的基础阶段。就英语来说，这个阶段要求掌握的词汇量为2400个（去掉遗忘，平均每个课时10个单词）。加上中学阶段已经学会的1600个单词，基础阶段结束时应掌握的词汇量为4000个。仅仅掌握4000个单词，能否看懂专业英文书刊呢？还不能。据统计，掌握4000个单词，阅读一般的英文科技文献，生词量仍将有6%左右，即平均每百词有六个生词，还不能自由阅读。国外的外语教学专家认为，生词量在3%以下，才能不借助词典，自由阅读。此时可以通过上下文的联系，把不认识的生词猜出来。那么，怎么样才能把6%的生词量降低到3%以下呢？自然，需要让学生增加一部分词汇积累。问题是，要增加多少单词？要增加哪一些单词？统计资料表明，在每一个专业的科技文献中，本专业最常用的科技术语大约只有几百个，而且它们在文献中重复出现的频率很高。因此，在已经掌握4000单词的基础上，在专业阅读阶段中，有针对性地通过大量阅读，扩充大约1000个与本专业密切有关的科技词汇，便可以逐步达到自由阅读本专业科技文献的目的。

　　早在八十年代中期，建设部系统院校外语教学研究会就组织编写了一套《土木建筑系列英语》，分八个专业，共12册。每个专业可选读其中的3、4册。那套教材在有关院校相应的专业使用多年，学生和任课教师反映良好。但是，根据当时的情况，那套教材定的起点较低（1000词起点），已不适合今天学生的情况。为此，在得到建设部人事教育劳动司的大力支持，并征得五个相关专业指导委员会同意之后，由建设部系统十几所院校一百余名外语教师和专业课教师按照统一的编写规划和要求，编写了这一套《建筑类专业英语》教材。

　　《建筑类专业英语》是根据国家教委颁发的《大学英语专业阅读阶段教学基本要求》编写的专业阅读教材，按照建筑类院校共同设置的五个较大的专业类别对口编写。五个专业类别为：建筑学与城市规划；建筑工程（即工业与民用建筑）；给水排水与环境保护；暖通、空调与燃气；建筑管理与财务会计。每个专业类别分别编写三册专业英语阅读教材，供该专业类别的学生在修完基础阶段英语后，在第五至第七学期专业阅读阶段使用，每学期一册。

　　上述五种专业英语教材语言规范，题材广泛，覆盖相关专业各自的主要内容：包括专业基础课，专业主干课及主要专业选修课，语言材料的难易度切合学生的实际水平；词汇以大学英语"通用词汇表"的 4000 个单词为起点，每个专业类别的三册书将增加 1000—1200 个阅读本专业必需掌握的词汇。本教材重视语言技能训练，突出对阅读、翻译和写作能力的培养，以求达到《大学英语专业阅读阶段教学基本要求》所提出的教学目标："通过指导学生阅读有关专业的英语书刊和文献，使他们进一步提高阅读和翻译科技资料的能力，并能以英语为工具获取专业所需的信息。"

《建筑类专业英语》每册 16 个单元，每个单元一篇正课文（TEXT），两篇副课文（Reading Material A & B），每个单元平均 2000 个词，三册 48 个单元，总共约有十万个词，相当于原版书三百多页。要培养较强的阅读能力，读十万个词的文献，是起码的要求。如果专业课教师在第六和第七学期，在学生通过学习本教材已经掌握了数百个专业科技词汇的基础上，配合专业课程的学习，再指定学生看一部分相应的专业英语科技文献，那将会既促进专业课的学习，又提高英语阅读能力，实为两得之举。

本教材不仅适用于在校学生，对于有志提高专业英语阅读能力的建筑行业广大在职工程技术人员，也是一套适用的自学教材。

建设部人事教育劳动司高教处和中国建设教育协会对这套教材的编写自始至终给予关注和支持；中国建筑工业出版社第五编辑室密切配合，参与从制定编写方案到审稿各个阶段的重要会议，给了我们很多帮助；在编写过程中，各参编学校相关专业的许多专家、教授对材料的选取、译文的审定都提出了许多宝贵意见，谨此致谢。

《建筑类专业英语》是我们编写对口专业阅读教材的又一次尝试，由于编写者水平及经验有限，教材中不妥之处在所难免，敬请广大读者批评指正。

《建筑类专业英语》
编审委员会

Contents

UNIT ONE
- Text   What Is Macroeconomics? 1
- Reading Material A   Nominal GNP, Real GNP, and the GNP Deflator 5
- Reading Material B   Recurring Business Cycles/Natural Real GNP 7

UNIT TWO
- Text   Building Economy (I) 11
- Reading Material A   Building Economy (II) 15
- Reading Material B   Building Economy (III) 16

UNIT THREE
- Text   Efficiency 18
- Reading Material A   Increasing Returns/Decreasing Returns 23
- Reading Material B   Demand and Supply Curves/Adjusting Capacity 24

UNIT FOUR
- Text   Cash Forecast 27
- Reading Material A   Profit-and-loss Forecast 31
- Reading Material B   Reporting 33

UNIT FIVE
- Text   The Successful Proposal 35
- Reading Material A   Insurance 40
- Reading Material B   Selecting a Method of Computerized Specifying 41

UNIT SIX
- Text   Architecture Is a Volatile Business 44
- Reading Material A   Staff-effect of Booms and Slumps 49
- Reading Material B   Professional Indemnity Insurance 51

UNIT SEVEN
- Text   Who Needs Quality Assurance? 53
- Reading Material A   What Should the Client Do? 58
- Reading Material B   Essential Features of QA 61

UNIT EIGHT
- Text   The Managerial Accountant's Role in Decision Making 64
- Reading Material A   The Master Budget: a Planning Tool 68
- Reading Material B   Operational Budgets 70

UNIT NINE
- Text   Housing Supply 72
- Reading Material A   Industrial Structure/Low Productivity Growth 77

Reading Material B Speculative Building/The Construction Firm ······ 79

UNIT TEN
Text   Construction ······ 82
Reading Material A Materials ······ 88
Reading Material B The Land Market and the Planning System ······ 90

UNIT ELEVEN
Text   Accounting ······ 93
Reading Material A Standards ······ 98
Reading Material B Nonstandards ······ 100

UNIT TWELVE
Text   Contractor's Duties ······ 102
Reading Material A Who Should Be Responsible for Defective Work? ······ 107
Reading Material B The Weather's Effect on Performance of Construction
                    Contracts ······ 108

UNIT THIRTEEN
Text   Plan Shape ······ 111
Reading Material A Size of Building ······ 115
Reading Material B Perimeter/Floor Area Ratios ······ 116

UNIT FOURTEEN
Text   The Investor's Objectives ······ 120
Reading Material A Risk and Return ······ 124
Reading Material B Reasons for Investing ······ 126

UNIT FIFTEEN
Text   Contracts (General, Identification of Project, Preparation of Scope) ······ 129
Reading Material A Selection of Contract Strategy ······ 134
Reading Material B Preparation of Tender Documents ······ 136

UNIT SIXTEEN
Text   Contractor/Sub-contractor Relationships (I) ······ 138
Reading Material A Contractor/Sub-contractor Relationships (II) ······ 143
Reading Material B Contractor/Sub-contractor Relationships (III) ······ 145
Appendix I   Vocabulary ······ 148
Appendix II   Translation for Reference ······ 155
Appendix III   Key to Exercises ······ 178

UNIT ONE

Text   What Is Macroeconomics?

[1]   Macroeconomics is concerned with the big economic issues that determine your own economic well-being as well as that of your family and everyone you know. Each of these issues involves the overall economic performance of the nation, rather than that of particular individuals.

[2]   For instance, do citizens find it easy or difficult to find jobs? On average, are prices rising rapidly, slowly, or not at all? How much total income is the nation producing, and how rapidly is total income growing year after year? Is the interest rate charged to borrow money high or low?① Is the government spending more than it collects in tax revenue? Is the nation as a whole accumulating assets in other countries or is it becoming more indebted to them?

[3]   Each of these six questions involves a central macroeconomic concept to which you will be introduced in this unit. Now let us take each one in turn and see how it affects everyday life:

[4]   1. The unemployment rate. The higher the overall unemployment rate, the harder it is for each individual who wants a job to find work. College seniors who want permanent jobs after graduation are likely to have more job offers if the national unemployment rate is low than high.② All adults fear a high unemployment rate. In "bad times" when the unemployment rate is high, crime, mental illness, and suicide also increase. It is no wonder that many people consider unemployment to be the single most important macroeconomic issue. And this is nothing new.

[5]   2. The inflation rate. A high inflation rate means that prices on average are rising rapidly, while a low inflation rate means that prices on average are rising slowly. An inflation rate of zero means that prices on average remain the same, month after month. Many people are affected when the economy shifts from a low to a high inflation rate, while a high inflation rate harms those who have saved in the past, it helps those who have borrowed.③ It is this capricious aspect of inflation, taking from some and giving to others, that makes people dislike inflation.④

[6]   3. Productivity growth. "Productivity" is the average amount per worker that a nation produces in total goods and services, the higher a nation's average productivity, the more there is to go around. The faster average productivity grows, the easier it is for each member of society to improve his or her standard of living. If the growth rate of productivity were zero, to have more houses and cars, we would have to sacrifice and build fewer hospitals or schools. Such an economy, with no productivity growth, has been called "the zero-sum society" because any additional good or service enjoyed by one person requires that something be taken away from someone else. Such a society, with constant sacrifice and strife, is not likely to be a

very pleasant place to live.

[7]   4. The interest rate. When interest rates are high, borrowing is expensive. The biggest losers are those who would like to become homeowners, since high interest rates boost the monthly payments on mortgages enough to make homeownership unaffordable for many people. College students and recent college graduates find that monthly payments on the new car of their dreams become too high, and they are forced to buy a smaller car, a used car, or perhaps no car at all. Changes in interest rates, whether up or down, disrupt financial planning for everyone, and create windfall gains and losses for savers, investors, and borrowers.

[8]   5. The government budget deficit. When the government spends more money than it takes in as tax revenue, it runs a deficit. People benefit from a budget deficit at the time it occurs, since they gain from the higher level of government spending (or lower taxes) than would occur if the budget were balanced.⑤ This is not a "free lunch," however, because eventually someone must pay the bill. Today's deficit will be paid, directly or indirectly, by citizens in the future, including college students now reading this text. Citizens will eventually "pay the bill" for today's government deficit through lower government spending that would have occurred otherwise, through higher taxes, or through lower income.

[9]   6. The foreign trade deficit. During the 1980s Americans purchased far more imports from foreign nations than we sold as exports. To pay for all these imports, Americans sold many assets to foreigners. By the end of the decade the United States had run up a debt to foreigners of hundreds of billions of dollars. The net result is to make tomorrow's citizens poorer by making foreign goods more expensive and by requiring that they pay a fraction of their future income as interest payments to foreigners.

New Words and Expressions

macroeconomics [ˌmækrəuiːkəˈnɔmiks]	n.	宏观经济学，大经济学
well-being	n.	福利
revenue * [ˈrevinjuː]	n.	收入，税收，收入总额
asset [ˈæset]	n.	[复] 资产，财产
indebted [inˈdetid]	a.	负债的
suicide [ˈsjuːisaid]	n.	自杀
inflation [inˈfleiʃən]	n.	通货膨胀
capricious [kəˈpriʃəs]	a.	反复无常的，无定见的
productivity [ˌprɔdʌkˈtiviti]	n.	生产率，生产能力
zero-sum [ˈziərəusʌm]	a.	一方得益引起另一方相应损失的
strife [straif]	n.	竞争，冲突
homeowner [ˈhəumˌəunə]	n.	房主
boost [buːst]	v.	提高
mortgage [ˈmɔːgidʒ]	n. & v.	抵押

homeownership [həumˈəunəʃip]	n.	房屋所有权
unaffordable [ˌʌnəˈfɔːdəbl]	a.	无法支付的，无法达到的
disrupt [disˈrʌpt]	v.	破坏，瓦解
windfall [ˈwindfɔːl]	n.	被风吹落的果实，（喻）收获，横财
budget [ˈbʌdʒit]	n.	预算
investor [inˈvestə]	n.	投资者
deficit [ˈdefisit]	n.	赤字，亏空
run up		欠下（许多债或帐）
the net result		最后结果

Notes

①句中 charged to borrow money 是过去分词短语作定语，修饰 rate。

②... if the national unemployment rate is low than high。

此句中 than 相当于 rather than 的用法，意思是"而不是"。

③句中 while 引导的是一个让步状语从句，it helps ... 中的 it 指 a high inflation rate。

④这是一个"it is... that..."强调句型，句中的 taking from some and giving to others 是 capricious aspect of inflation 的同位语。

⑤... since they gain from the higher level of government spending or lower taxes than would occur if the budget were balanced。

句中 than 引导的是一个省略的比较状语从句，从句中省略了主语 what，同样的用法还有本段的最后一句，... through lower government spending than would have occurred otherwise ...。

Exercises

Reading Comprehension

Ⅰ. Choose the best answer.

1. If the national unemployment rate is low, college students
   A. have permanent jobs.
   B. want more jobs.
   C. have more chances to find jobs.
   D. want more permanent job offers.

2. All adults are afraid of a high unemployment rate because
   A. the higher the unemployment rate the more the crime mentalillness and suicide cases.
   B. many people consider unemployment to be the single mostimportant macroeconomic issue.

C. they probably have too much more permanent job offers to choose if the unemployment rate is high.

D. it is more difficult for them to find jobs if the unemployment rate is high.

3. Changes in interest rates from low to high create gains for _____.

   A. savers

   B. borrowers

   C. investors

   D. all of them

4. If the government runs a deficit, which statement is not true? A. The goverment spends more money than it takes in.

   B. People benefit from the deficit at the time it occurs.

   C. Citizens will eventually pay the deficit.

   D. The government will try to pay the deficit and balance it.

5. Which statement is not true according to the text?

   A. Macroeconomics is the study of economic performance of particular individuals.

   B. Some people cannot enjoy more goods and have to sacrifice in the zero-sum society.

   C. people dislike inflation because it means taking from some and giving to others.

   D. Fewer people borrow money when interest rates are high.

II. Match Column A with Column B according to the text.

A	B
1. low inflation rate	a. People have to constantly sacrifice and strife
2. lower productivity	b. That will eventually make tomorrow's citizens poorer
3. zero productivity growth rate	c. Prices on average are rising slowly
4. high taxes	d. Today's deficit will be paid by citizens in the future through …
5. high debt to foreigners	e. The average amount per worker prodnces in total goods and services decreases

Vocabulary

I. Fill in the blanks with the words and expressions given below. Change the form if necessary.

> strife, accumulate, disrupt, go around, mortgage

1. She could not drive to work because snow _____ in the driveway to a depth of five

feet.
  2. Telephone service _____ for hours because of the heavy flood.
  3. He needs money and raises a _____ on his house from a bank.
  4. The market economy is certainly to cause severe _____ of the marketplace.
  5. There are so many people that we have not enough food _____.
Ⅱ. Match the words in Column A with their corresponding definitions in Column B.

A	B
1. capricious	a. increase or raise
2. revenue	b. deprive oneself of something for the sake of another person, purpose or ideal
3. boost	c. changeable
4. deficit	d. a financial accounting loss
5. sacrifice	e. the income of a government from taxation, customs or other sources

Reading Material A

Nominal GNP, Real GNP, and the GNP Deflator

To understand the behavior of the six key macroecomomic aggregates we need a measure of the size of the economy as a whole. Probably the most frequently used abbreviation in macroeconomics is GNP, which stands for gross national product. This measure of the economy's overall size is defined as the value of all currently produced goods and services sold on the market during a particular time interval. ① GNP can be most easily thought of as the total amount of current production.

Economists compute GNP by a process of adding up all the different types of current production. The market value of the actual amount of production is called nominal GNP. The word nominal means the actual amount produced at current prices. Nominal amounts are not very useful for economic analysis because they can increase either when people buy more physical goods and services-more cars, steaks, and haircuts-or when prices rise.

Are we better off if we spend more money? Or have price increases chewed up all our higher spending, leaving us no better off than before? Changes in nominal magnitudes cannot answer these questions; they hide more than they reveal. So economists concentrate on changes in real magnitudes, which eliminate the influence of year-to-year changes in prices and reflect true changes in the number, size and quality of items purchased. ②

Nominal GNP suffers the defects of any nominal magnitude, since its increases could reflect either increases in real production or in prices. To focus on changes in production and eliminate the influence of changing prices, we need a measure of real gross national product, or real GNP. Like any real magnitude, real GNP is expressed in the prices of an arbitrarily chosen "base year." The official measures of GNP in the United States use 1982 as the base year. Real GNP for every year, whether 1929 or 1990. is measured by taking the production of that particular year expressed at the constant prices of 1982.

Is real GNP in a particular year larger or smaller than nominal GNP? The answer depends on whether prices in that particular year on average were higher or lower than in 1982. Since prices usually increase each year, nominal GNP is higher than real GNP for year after 1982. Similarly, nominal GNP is lower than real GNP for years before 1982. You can see this regular pattern in Figure 1-1, which displays nominal and real GNP for each year since 1870.

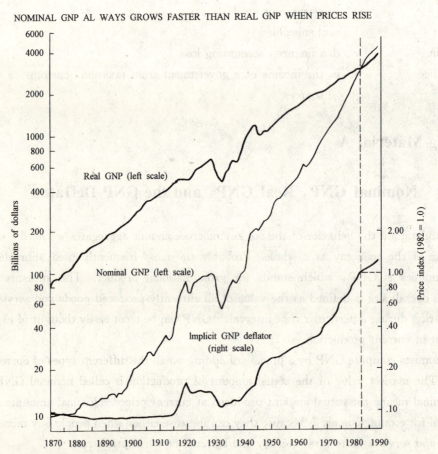

Figure 1-1 Nominal GNP, Real GNP, and the Implicit GNP Deflator, 1870~1989

Notice how the nominal GNP line lies below the real GNP line before 1982 but lies above the real GNP line after 1982. This reflects the fact that the current prices used to measure no-minal GNP were lower before 1982 than the 1982 prices used to measure real GNP. After 1982 the current prices used to measure nominal GNP were higher than the 1982 prices used to measure real GNP. Notice how the nominal GNP line crosses the real GNP line in 1982, the same year that the GNP deflator attains the value of 1.00. This occurs because in 1982 (and no other year) the prices used to measure nominal GNP and real GNP are the same.

Later on we will consider other real magnitudes, such as real consumption and the real money supply. An alternative label for real magnitudes is "constant-dollar," in contrast to nominal magnitudes, which are usually called "current-dollar".

The ratio of nominal to real GNP is called the implicit GNP deflator. The deflator tells us the ratio of prices actually charged in any single year (say, 1929) to the prices charged in the base year 1982.③ How is the implicit GNP deflator related to the "inflation rate," the second of the six central macroeconomic concepts? The inflation rate is the rate of change of the implicit GNP deflator.

The relationship between the implicit GNP deflator and the inflation rate can be remembered easily, When the implicit GNP deflator is rising, the inflation rate is positive. When the implicit GNP deflator is unchanged, the inflation rate is zero, And when the implicit GNP deflator is falling (a rarity), the inflation rate is negative.

An inflation is said to occur when the inflation rate is positive for a sustained period, that is, when there is a sustained upward movement in the implicit GNP deflator. A deflation is said to occur when the inflation rate is negative for a sustained period. that is, when there is a sustained downward movement in the implicit GNP deflator.

Notes

①这种对整体经济规模的衡量就是指在一个特定的时间阶段内所有在市场上销售的近期生产的产品和服务的价值。
②于是经济学家们注重真实数量的变化，这种变化能够说明在价格上年与年之间的影响并且反映出对所购物品在数量、体积及质量上的真实变化。
③这种紧缩通货比率告诉我们任何一年（比如说 1929 年）的价格同 1982 年这一基准年的价格比。

Reading Material B

Recurring Business Cycles/Natural Real GNP

Recurring Business Cycles

Throughout history the economy has experienced business cycles, alternating periods of good times and bad times. Look again at Figure 1-1 and find the thick black real GNP line. Notice that real GNP becomes larger over time, but also exhibits up-and-down wiggles. These wiggles represent the business cycles that have recurred throughout history, culminating in the most extreme business cycle of all, the Great Depression of 1929~1933 when real GNP declined by 30 percent in one continuous and catastrophic downward movement.①

The distinguishing characteristic of business cycles is their pervasive character,[2] which affects many different types of economic activity at the same time. Business cycles are recurrent but not periodic. This means that they recur again and again but are not always the same length. Business cycles in the past have ranged in length from one to twelve years.

Figure 1-2 illustrates two successive business cycles in real GNP. The high point in real GNP in each cycle is called the business cycle peak. The low point is called the trough. The period between peak and trough is called a recession. After the recession comes the expansion, which continues until the following peak.

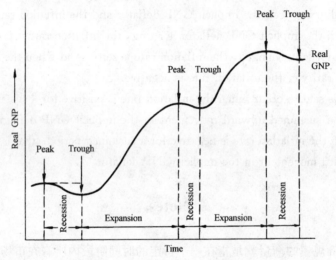

Figure 1-2 A Succession of Cycles

Although a simplification, Figure 1-2 contains two realistic elements that have been common to most real-world business cycles. First, the expansions last longer than the recessions. This occurs because on average real GNP is growing over time, so each successive peak is higher than the last peak. Second, the two business cycles illustrated in the figure differ in length. Since World War II, business-cycle expansions have been as short as one year (July 1980 to July 1981) and as long as nine years (February 1961 to December 1969).

Real GNP: Actual and Natural

Between a high production level that causes the inflation rate to speed up, and a low production level that causes the inflation rate to slow down, there is some desirable compromise level that keeps the inflation rate constant. This intermediate level of real GNP has been called "natural," a situation in which there is no tendency for inflation to accelerate or decelerate.

Figure 1-3 illustrates the relationship between actual real GNP, natural real GNP, and the rate of inflation. In the upper frame the red line is actual real GNP, exhibiting exactly the same business cycles as in Figure 1-2. In the lower frame is shown the inflation rate.[3] The thin dashed vertical lines connect the two frames. The first dashed vertical line marks time period t_0 Notice in the bottom frame that the inflation rate is constant at t_0.

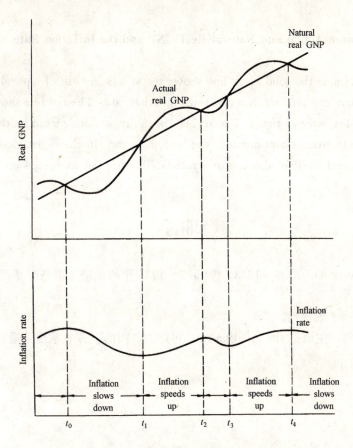

Figure 1-3 Why Too Much Real GNP is Undesirable

By definition, natural real GNP is equal to actual real GNP when the inflation rate is constant. Thus in the upper frame at t_0 the red actual real GNP line is crossed by a black natural real GNP line. To the right of t_0 actual real GNP falls below natural real GNP, and we see in the bottom frame that inflation slows down. This continues until time period t_1, when actual real GNP recovers to once again equal natural real GNP. Here the inflation rate stops falling and is constant for a moment before it begins to rise.

This cycle repeats again and again. Only when actual real GNP is equal to natural real GNP is the inflation rate constant. For this reason. natural real GNP is a natural or compromise level to be singled out for special attention. During a period of low actual real GNP, designated by the gray area, the inflation rate slows down. During a period of high actual real GNP, designated by the pink area, the inflation rate accelerates. Sometimes the condition of excessive actual real GNP is called "an overheated economy", a designation that you can link to the pink area on the diagram.

Basic Business Cycle Concepts The red real GNP line exhibits a typical succession of business cycles. The highest point rea-ched by real GNP in each cycle is called the "peak" and the lowest point the "trough". The "recession" is the period bet-ween peak and trough, the "expansion" the period be-tween the trough and the next peak.

The Relation between Actual and Natural Real GNP and the Inflation Rate

In the upper frame the solid black line shows the steady growth of natural real GNP-the amount the economy can produce at a const-ant inflation rate. The red line shows the path of actual real GNP, the same as that in Figure 1-2. in the region designated by the gray area in the top frame, so inflation slows down in the bottom frame. In the region designated by the pink area. actual real GNP is abovenatural real GNP. so inflation speeds up in the bottom frame.

Notes

①the Great Depression of 1929~1933。指 1929~1933 年的经济大萧条时期，即资本主义世界的经济危机。
②pervasive character 渗透性。
③这是一个倒装句，主语是 the inflation rate 句意为：图的下方表示出了通货膨胀率。

UNIT TWO

Text   Building Economy (Ⅰ)

[1]   Building is one of the most important activities in any economy. A large part of the national resources are usually used in the construction and maintenance of buildings and buildings play an important part both in production and in providing services to the community. Clearly, it is important that good value should be obtained from the resources used. It is not surprising that building and buildings should be subject to frequent criticism. Unfortunately much of this criticism is ill-informed. All too frequently the complex of factors relating to building is ignored and as a result many of the recommendations are of little value or even damaging.

[2]   While many products, and the industries which produce them, have come to fruition in half a century, building and buildings as they are known today have been developing throughout recorded history. Their development has taken place both in time and geographically. The conical hut of branches is both the origin of contemporary building forms and in some parts of the world a contemporary building form itself.① While the ordinary citizen built in mud, wattle and timber, the church and state built in brick and stone. Naturally, it is only examples of the monumental building of the church and state which survive today. However, while the buildings of the ordinary citizen have not endured, the history of the buildings is largely discernible in the contemporary forms of the less developed peoples of the world.② A study of the relationships between the forms of construction and the contemporary conditions, both in the past and currently in other countries, is of assistance in obtaining an understanding of the current problems of the building economy.

[3]   Where the economy is poor the ordinary citizen builds for himself and professional builders are employed only by the church and state. Thus the two kinds of buildings, domestic and monumental, tend to develop in different ways. Domestic buildings tend to be built by the house-holders and their neighbours from such materials as lie ready to hand on the site. At first, materials are used in their crude state, but gradually more effort is made to fashion the materials to fit together to provide shelters of a more convenient form and better able to provide protection from the elements. Naturally, people who only occasionally take part in an activity cannot acquire the skill and knowledge of people practising full time. The skill of the professional is passed on from one generation to the next and is cross fertilised by contact with builders from other areas. Professional building tends to advance much more rapidly than the building of the householder. As society becomes more wealthy and sophisticated, the proportion of people satisfied with shelters they can build themselves and with the need and time to erect and maintain their own shelters declines and more and more people employ professional builders.③ Thus the evolution of building and buildings is a result of the interaction between materials, skills and the external economies.

[4]   In many ways professional buildings have not changed radically over the last 2000 years. The houses of the wealthy Romans were not dissimilar to houses of today. The engineering structures of the Romans were as large and as ambitious as those of today. On the other hand, the range of materials available today is far wider and the knowledge of their properties is greater. As a result the materials can be used more adventurously and economically. Moreover, the range of mechanical aids is far greater and so less labour and time needs to be used. The most significant changes in buildings lie in the range of engineering services now incorporated in them.

[5]   While in the more developed countries professional building accounts for most of the building work, the reverse is true in the less developed countries. Naturally, the owner-built dwellings usually lack the amenities expected in western type homes, especially the mechanical engineering and plumbing services. One of the economic problems in developing countries is to determine the best point at which to change from the use of self-built constructions, based on local and usually short life materials, to professional building based on manufactured materials.

[6]   While in sophisticated societies the ordinary citizen usually looks to the professional builder for major construction work, he frequently undertakes minor works and maintenance himself. This trend tends to grow in societies in which the cost of labour is growing rapidly relative to the cost of materials and components, and net after tax earnings, and in which changes in components and a growing availability of cheap small power tools reduces both the skill content and arduousness of the tasks.④

New Words and Expressions

fruition [fruˈiʃən]	n.	实现；完成
conical [ˈkɔnikəl]	a.	圆锥形的
wattle [ˈwɔtl]	n.	枝条；篱笆条
timber * [timbə]	n.	木料；木材
monumental [mɔnjuːˈmentəl]	a.	纪念的；巨大的
discernible [diˈsəːnəbl]	a.	看得清的；辨别得出的
ready to hand		就在手边的；随手可得的
elements	n.	（复）风雨，自然力
householder [ˈhaushəud]	n.	占有房子的人；住户；户主
pass on		传给（另外的人），传下去
cross-fertilise	v.	（植）使异花受精；（喻）使相互补充而得益
radically [ˈrædikəli]	a.	根本地，基本地；激进地
ambitious [æmˈbiʃəs]	a.	炫耀的；有雄心的
adventurously [ədˈventʃərəsli]	a.	带有冒险性地；带有危险性地
incorporate * [inˈkɔːpəreit]	v.	使具体化，体现；合并；纳入，结合
amenity [əˈmiːniti]	n.	令人愉快的东西，（环境、房屋）舒适

plumbing ['plʌmiŋ]	n.	管子工作，铅管业；(总称)管件
look to sb. for		指望某人……
component [kəm'pəunənt]	n.	构件，组成部分
availability [əˌveilə'biliti]	n.	可得性，可得到的东西
arduousness ['ɑːdjuəsnis]	n.	艰巨，艰苦

Notes

①注意 both ... and ... 的搭配关系，所连接的两部分都是句子的表语。

②while 的意思为"虽然、尽管"，在此句中引导让步状语从句。

③这是一个复合句，主句为一个并列句，declines 及 employ 分别是并列句中两个分句的谓语。satisfied with shelters 为过去分词短语作定语修饰 people，with the need and time 为介词短语做定语修饰 shelters。

④此句中 in which ... ，and in which 分别是两个并列的定语从句，修饰 societies。
在第二个定语从句中谓语 reduces 后的两个宾语由 both ... and ... 所连接。

Exercises

Reading Comprehension

I. Choose the best answer.

1. The domestic and monumental buildings tend to develop in different way in places where
   A. there exist both the poor and the rich.
   B. the economy is poor.
   C. there are not professional builders.
   D. there are not building materials.

2. Which is untrue to professional buildings?
   A. Professional buildings have changed a lot over years.
   B. Professional buildings developed faster than domestic buildings.
   C. More and more people became satisfied with professional buildings.
   D. Professional buildings can only be built by skilled professionals.

3. Most buildings as the owner-built dwellings in the less developed countries usually
   A. lack mechanical engineering and plumbing services.
   B. are built with local and short life materials.
   C. are built with fashioned manufactured materials.
   D. both A and B.

4. In which aspect are the professional buildings not superior to those of the wealthy Romans?

A. Larger and more ambitious structures.
   B. Wider material supplies and greater knowledge of their properties.
   C. More adventurously and economically used materials.
   D. Greater range of mechanical aids and less labour and time cost.
5. In societies where the cost of labor grows faster than that of materials and components, the ordinary people usually
   A. have their buildings completely built by the professional builders.
   B. build their buildings themselves.
   C. have major construction work done by professional builders and do the small maintenance work themselves.
   D. build the main structure of their buildings themselves and have minor maintenance work done by professional builders.

II. Match Column A with Column B according to the text.

A	B
1. domestic buildings	a. usually changed little over thousand of years and were built in brick, stone and even better materials by professionals
2. professional buildings	b. usually lack such amenities as mechanical engineering and plumbing services and were built in such local short life materials as mud, wattle and timber
3. buildings in developed countries	c. usually had large and ambitious structures
4. buildings in less developed countries	d. usually were different from place to place and built by the house-holders and their neighbours from ready-to-hand materials
5. buildings of the wealthy Romans	e. usually have better plumbing services and are built in manufactured materials by professional builders

Vocabulary

I. Fill in the blanks with the words given below. Change the form if neccessary.

> interact, endure, arduous, maintenance, manufacture

1. Machine concrete mixing replaces labour on a very _____ task.
2. However, increasingly standard units of buildings are being _____ for housing, industrial and storage purposes, and to some extent for educational, social and office purposes.
3. All things are interrelated and _____ on each other.

4. The instruction book gives full information on the operation and _____ of the new machine.
5. They had spent 3 days in the desert without water, and could not _____ much longer.

II. Match the words in Column A with their corresponding definitions in Column B.

A	B
1. undertake	a. modern; of the present
2. monumental	b. can be seen or made out through any of the senses.
3. discernible	c. make sth. a part of a group; include
4. contemporary	d. of great and lasting worth
5. incorporate	e. take up a position; start on work

Reading Material A

Building Economy (II)

The evaluation of buildings depends on whether they are required as a means of production or for consumption in the productive sector of the economy a building is just another factor of production; it has no value in itself but only in as far as it provides shelter for a productive or distributive process or generates an income.① it is a cost of production and has a precise money value. Consumers value buildings for themselves; for the satisfactions which they provide.② Many of these statisfactions are personal and subjective, and no precise objective valuation is possible.

Building and works may be supplied either "bespoke", or "off-the peg"; the former are designed especially to meet the expressed needs of a particular client, while the latter are available either as speculatively erected buildings for sale, or as standard units for erection on the clients' sites. Most public, commercial and industrial buildings are of the first class, while most private housing is of the second class. However, increasingly standard units of buildings are being manufactured for housing, industrial and storage purposes and to some extent for educational, social and office purposes. On the other hand, civil engineering works are usually designed to the requirements of an individual client.

Bespoke buildings are mostly designed and erected by two separate groups of people, the materials being supplied by a further group. The design group, which may consist of several separate groups, usually under the co-ordination of an architect, are professionals, who act for the client on a fee basis. The contracting group, which may consist of a dozen or more separate firms, work for profit and generally secure the contracts on competitive basis. Again, the suppliers of the materials and components consist of many separate firms competing for the business. Sometimes they compete with designs as well as with the supply of the components.

There is less division of responsibility in the case of off-the-peg buildings. The designer is employed by the contractor; often he is on his staff. Frequently, especially where the buildings are supplied in the form of standard units, the contractor also manufactures the major material or component. Thus in such cases the designer-producer relationship is similar to that in manufacturing industry, where the manufacturer is responsible for both design and production.

However, whichever type of building is used the contractor is largely an erector, an assembler of the products of other industries. Except for buildings based on unprocessed materials, about half the cost of a building is the cost of the materials used in its construction. This proportion rises as less use is made of the products of the extractive industries and more use is made of large prefabricated components. ③

Notes

①建筑本身没什么价值，只有在为某一生产或是分配过程提供场地保障或者带来收入时才有价值。
②消费者为自己评价建筑物的价值。根据建筑物提供的条件的满意程度去估算建筑物的价值。
③随着越来越少地使用采掘业所产的粗制产品而更多地利用大批的预制构件，这一比例也随着上升。

Reading Material B

Building Economy (Ⅲ)

Many observers have felt that traditional building, involving as it does the joining together of a large number of small units, must be basically inefficient.① Building has been critically compared with the factory industries and with the success they have achieved in mechanisation, in replacing craft process with machines and with semi-skilled labour and with their success with large scale methods. There have been various attempts to try to emulate these methods in building. Broadly, these attempts have taken four forms; prefabrication, system building, mechanisation, and the rationalisation of the erection process.

Prefabrication has developed along two lines: in the form of standard as compared with purpose-made components. The use of standard components has been developing steadily over the last half century. More and more items of joinery and metal goods are purchased ready made; plasterboard and plaster panels are replacing wet plaster; electrical and plumbing systems can be obtained with units cut to size and ready for installation. The development of systems of construction has naturally been most noticeable in those fields in which a standardised product is acceptable, for example, housing and schools. Some of these systems have been based on interlocking units which form a load-bearing structure; the units vary in size from

16

traditionally sized building blocks to room-sized units. Other systems have been built around a frame hung with a light cladding material.

Mechanisation has mainly developed in four directions: earthmovement, materials handling, concrete mixing and powered hand tools to assist manual tasks. The greatest success has perhaps been obtained in earthmoving, where the power and endurance of the machine in relation to its cost is so much greater than that of the man it replaces. Materials handling has developed in step with the growth in size of building units.② Machine concrete mixing also replaces labour on a very arduous task. No real success has so far been achieved in mechanising craft processes, but the development of powered hand tools, jigs and simply installed prefabricated components has reduced both the skill content and the physical difficulties of much craft work. This tends to reduce the intensity of skill training necessary for craftsmen and increases the feasibility of training craftsmen able to handle a much wider range of tasks, reducing the number of separate operatives necessary for carrying out building operations.

The development of prefabricated methods of building and of mechanisation has necessarily been accompanied by the rationalisation of the erection process. This starts with the study of the flow of work on the site. Up to a point a building job can be preplanned so that all the operations can be timed to fit into one continuous sequence of operations. To be successful such planning must be accompanied by very good organisation so that all the various types of labour and materials are brought on to the site at the right time. The full potential of such methods cannot be realised unless the design and building methods are examined together. The substitution of certain materials or certain design features may greatly simplify the whole construction process, especially where complete operations can be eliminated. Thus successful rationalisation in the building industry requires an examination of the design and construction together and their development as an organic whole.③

Notes

① 许多评论家认为，那些传统建筑，即由大量的小部件构成的建筑本质上来说肯定是低效率的。
② 随着建筑构件体积的增大，原材料的搬运工作也同步得到发展。
③ 这样，在建筑业方面，成功的合理化方案要求将建筑的设计和建造以及他们的改进情况作为一个有机的整体来检查。

UNIT THREE

Text   Efficiency

[1]   The efficiency of the building industry and hence the cost of building depends on five main factors: the clients, the designers, the contractors, the producers of materials, and the economic and institutional environment. The client's contribution lies in his skill in specifying his needs prior to the preparation of the design and in assessing the value of the solutions put forward by the designer.① The designer occupies the central role. His contribution lies in meeting the needs of the client with a solution economic to construct and to operate. He must thus take account of the problems likely to arise in the erection of the building and of the extent to which materials and components are or can be made available.② designers can have a larger influence on cost than either contractors or producers of materials since they determine the overall building and can reduce cost not only by using materials to the best advantage and in a way which simplifies erection but also by planning to meet the needs in a smaller space and by enclosing it in the minimum area of walls and roof.③ The contractors' contribution to cost reduction lies in the efficiency with which they assemble the building. This is not just a question of speed but of a proper balance between labour and organisation. The producers of materials can assist in cheapening the product by improving the efficiency of their process of extracting, manufacturing and distributing the materials and components. The economic and institutional environment affects efficiency by the way in which it facilitates the design and construction process and by the restrictions it imposes upon the industry.④

[2]   Most clients are involved in the exercise of their function only occasionally and must rely heavily on the skill of the designer in assessing the nature of their needs and the value of the solutions put forward.

[3]   The design of a building, particularly today, is a very complex problem, demanding a greater breadth of knowledge than most other design problems. The complexity arises from the size of a building and the number of purposes it serves, from the number and range of services to be provided and from the range of materials and methods of construction which are possible. Design economy can only be achieved through an understanding of the fundamental user requirements and an ability to compare the ultimate cost consequences of the many possible solutions. The designs of different components of a building interact with each other and with the ways the building can be used, and affect the costs of running it and of operating within it.⑤ Few people can be experts in all the facets of the design of a building and its services but the leader of the design team must at least have an overall appreciation of the problems of all the disciplines.

[4]   The development of new materials and new building techniques and the increase in the complexity of the services provided in a building has added to the erection problems as well as

to the design problems. ⑥ Not so long ago the range of materials and techniques of construction were so limited that building craftsmen could set out and erect buildings from the information given in simple outline drawings. The services to be fitted were few and simple and a contractor could generally understand the whole building process. Today the possible forms of construction are extensive and many of the services are very complex. Detailed drawings and often specialised knowledge are necessary. The traditional crafts tend to play a role of reduced importance and more and more specialist workers are employed. The more complicated forms of building and the demand for more rapid erection necessitate careful site planning and organisation; it is no longer adequate to follow through the natural sequence of trades. ⑦ Moreover, the improvements in the standards of living and of general working conditions, and the tendency to labour shortages in many of the more advanced countries, have resulted in a need for better organisation and labour conditions and for higher pay. ⑧ The greater the relative cost of site labour the greater the need for labour to be used efficiently.

[5] Traditional building materials are generally bulky and heavy, and variable in shape and size. While cheap in themselves they are often expensive to use. Techniques of using them have been evolved. Even so, such materials often have a limited technical performance. Moreover, being bulky and heavy they are costly to transport. At a time when transport was relatively undeveloped, and in countries where this is still so, building materials are not generally much used outside their locality of origin. Where such conditions pertain the forms of construction are limited and building is usually expensive. The development of cheap transport results in a cheapening of materials and increases the range available. It both encourages the spread and standardisation of existing materials and favours the development of easily transportable materials. ⑨

[6] New materials, often developed in other fields, have been found which provide greater flexibility in use and which are lighter and more uniform than traditional materials. Such materials often enable a greater range of problems to be solved and are often cheaper for their purpose than traditional materials. Frequently, however, the newer materials do not combine easily with the traditional ones.

New Words and Expressions

client * ['klaiənt]	n.	业主
contractor * [kən'træktə]	n.	承包商
institutional [insti'tjuʃənəl]	a.	惯例的；制度上的；公共机构的
take account of		考虑……
erection [i'rekʃən]	n.	建造；建立；安装
extract [iks'trækt]	v.	选取；提取
facilitate [fə'siliteit]	v.	使容易；促进
complexity [kɔmp'leksiti]	n.	复杂（性），复杂的事物

interact *	[intərˈækt]	v.	相互作用，相互影响
facet	[ˈfæsit]	n.	（题目，思想等）某一方面
craftsman	[ˈkrɑːftsmən]	n.	手艺人，工匠
necessitate *	[niˈsesiteit]	v.	使成为必要（需）
be adequate to do			适于做……，足以做……
bulky *	[ˈbʌlki]	a.	庞大的，笨大的
locality *	[ləuˈkæliti]	n.	位置，地点，所在地
pertain	[pəːˈtein]	v.	适合；关于；属于
standardisation *	[ˌstændədaiˈzeiʃən]	n.	标准化，规格化
transportable	[trænsˈpɔːtəbl]	a.	可运输的，可移动的
flexibility *	[ˌfleksəˈbiliti]	n.	柔（韧）性，灵活性

Notes

①句中"in specifying..."和"in assessing"为两个并列的介词短语，在句中作定语修饰 skill。"put forward by the designer"为过去分词短语，作定语修饰 solutions。

②句中 of the problems... 和 of the extent... 是两个等同成分。likely to arise... 是定语，修饰 problems。to which materials... 为定语从句，修饰 the extent，其结构相当于 materials are available or materials can be made available。

③句中 since 引导的是一个原因状语从句，determine 和 can reduce 为从句中两个并列谓语。not only by using... but also by planning... and by enclosing... 都为方式状语。

④句中 by the way... 和 by the restrictions 是两个并列状语修饰谓语动词 affects。两个状语中都有定语从句，分别修饰 the way 和 the restrictions。

⑤句中 interact 和 affect 为两个并列谓语。with each other 和 with the way... 是同等成分。of running it 和 of operating within it 为介词短语作定语，修饰 costs。

⑥句中 the development... 和 the increase... 为两个并列主语。of new... and new... 为介词短语作定语，修饰第一个主语。过去分词短语 provided... 作定语，修饰 services。

⑦句中 the more... and the demand for... 为两个并列主语，necessitate 为本句的谓语动词。

⑧the improvements... 和 the tendency... 是两个并列主语。have resulted in 是句子的谓语。

⑨句中 both... and... 连接两个并列谓语 encourages 和 favours。

Exercises

Reading Comprehension

I. Choose the best answer.

1. The erection and the design of buildings become more and more complex because
   A. the services in a building are more complex.
   B. the contractor and crafts cannot agree with each other about the erection and design.
   C. the new materials develop so fast.
   D. the building techniques develop quickly.

2. Which of the following statements is not true?
   A. The range of materials and techniques of construction today is large.
   B. The possible forms of construction are complicated and extensive.
   C. The more rapid erection of building demands careful site planning and organization.
   D. More and more traditional workers are employed because they still tend to play an important role.

3. Which of the following doesn't lead to the high labour cost?
   A. The improvement in the standards of living.
   B. The shortage of labour resources.
   C. The improvement of general working condition.
   D. The greater efficient use of labour.

4. Traditional building materials are often expensive to use probably because _____.
   A. they themselves are expensive
   B. they are costly to transport
   C. they have a limited technical performance
   D. B or C

5. Compared with traditional materials _____.
   A. new materials are cheaper
   B. new materials are lighter
   C. new materials often have a greater range in use
   D. all of the above

II. Match Column A with Column B according to the text.

A	B
factors	contribution or influence
1. the producers of material	a. meeting the needs of a client with a solution economic to construct and to operate and taking account of the problems likely to arise in the erection of the building

2. the clients

b. cheapening the product by improving the efficiency of their process of extracting, manufacturing and distributing the materials and components

3. the contractors

c. assembling the building efficiently to reduce the building cost

4. the economic and institutional environment

d. the skill in specifying the needs prior to the preparation of the design and in assessing the value of the solutions put forward by the designer

5. the designer

e. affecting efficiency by the way in which it facilitates the design and construction process and by the restrictions it imposes upon industry.

Vocabulary

I. Fill in the blanks with the words given below. Change the form if necessary.

| simplify, | extract, | facilitate, | assess, | necessitate |

1. The development of wheeled vehicles _____ the transport of agricultural and industrial products from one region to another.
2. The high density vertical city（立体城市）_____ the lightweight steel cagestructure, the elevator and the energy supply system.
3. It is not easy to _____ gold from rocks, but it doesn't follow that gold is expensive.
4. Try to _____ the explanation in the book for the children, for it is for adults.
5. A good client can _____ the value of a design and also the cost of a building according to the design.

II. Match the words in Column A with their corresponding definitions in Column B.

A	B
1. component	a. belong to, have a connection with
2. consequence	b. the same in every way
3. pertain	c. part
4. bulky	d. large
5. uniform	e. result

Reading Material A

Increasing Returns/Decreasing Returns

Increasing Returns

Up to a point the addition of a factor of production can result in an increase in returns more than proportional to the increase in the factor. ① This can occur for a number of reasons such as an ability to make a better use of available skills, a better use of an indivisible factor of production and to substitute better skills or capital equipment. Some examples will clarify the principle. An operative working single handed to build a brick wall will need to carry out several separate operations such as assembling and placing materials, mixing mortar, laying bricks and measuring. The skill and rhythm of each operation will be reduced by frequent breaks to carry out the other operations. If several men are employed each can specialise in a particular skill and tool, and achieve greater productivity. At the same time less time will be spent on non-productive work. If the job is large enough together they should turn out more work than if each were working singly. ②

Again two or three men often cannot utilise the full potential of even a small concrete mixer or crane. If more people can be used on the job, potential can be used more fully and costs per unit output generally reduced.

The output of most types of plant increases more than in proportion to its costs as its size is increased : the economics of scale. Costs per unit can therefore be reduced generally by using a larger size of plant but only if the full potential can be used over a long period.

Again a larger scale of operation may justify use of a higher type of skill or more sophisticated type of plant reducing the unit costs of employing operative skills.

Decreasing Returns

Increasing the scale of operation beyond a certain point may result in decreasing returns. This could occur, either if so many units of production were applied to a fixed unit that utilisation per unit was reduced or if overhead costs were pushed up. While a larger gang could make a better use of the output of a concrete mixer and utilise more of its potential, if there were too many in the gang they would tend to impede each other, perhaps in moving concrete from the mixer to the job or in pouring the concrete itself. Clearly the job needs to be large enough to enable a larger scale of operation to be economic. It is not, however, sufficient to limit consideration to the operation itself. It is necessary to balance the economies of each of the factors of production. It might, for example, be more economic to use a smaller and less efficient machine for the operation, pushing up prime costs, in order to have a machine which could be more intensively used on the site and in the firm, reducing plant overheads by more than prime costs were increased.

Overheads generally raise as the scale of the operation and firm rises. The economies of the scale of management are generally much less than of plant. As the scale of operations is increased more managerial and supervisory staff are generally required. These additional costs may be worth incurring if as a result prime costs can be reduced.

Land development provides an interesting example of the operation of increasing and decreasing returns. The total costs of providing a dwelling declines as the number on a given site is increased as long as no change is made in the form in which the dwellings are provided. If the limit in the number of houses which can be accommodated on the site is exceeded and high flatted blocks are used to achieve a higher density, the construction costs of a dwelling rise faster than the decline in land costs per unit, so that total costs per dwelling rise.

Notes

① 在一个生产环节上，每增加一个生产要素所能带来的利润的增长，比相应的要素本身的增长所产生的利润要多。

② 如果将工作的各个方面加起来是十分庞杂的，那么他们要完成的工作任务就会比每人独自干一份活要多。

Reading Material B

Demand and Supply Curves/Adjusting Capacity

Demand and Supply Curves

Generally the price customers are prepared to pay, the demand price, tends to fall with the volume available. This is because marginal satisfactions per unit acquired tend to fall. For example, a single hammer is necessary to a carpenter, two hammers might be a convenience, each further hammer would tend to be less useful. If the price was thought to be high he would equip himself with only one hammer, at a lower price he might purchase two; the lower the price the greater the purchase would tend to be. The demand price for all the units purchased at the same time is the price of the commodity only just worth purchasing. The total quantity sold depends on the price asked. Normally this would not be less than the marginal cost of production. The best returns would be made when the marginal cost of production were at a minimum and also equaled the demand price at that level of output (Fig. 3-1). If a higher price were demanded less would be sold and marginal costs would be higher. If more were put on the market the offer price would tend to be less and marginal costs higher. Except where the seller has a monopoly he cannot limit supply and must take the demand price as fixed and will hence try to produce and sell the quantity for which his marginal costs are at a minimum.

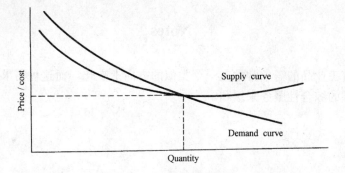

Fig. 3-1 Building Economy

In the above discussion long time costs and prices have been discussed. Costs have been taken to include normal profit, one that makes it just worthwhile to incur the risks of production. Prices will tend to be greater or less when demand and supply are out of balance. If demand increases purchasers will be prepared to pay a higher price and prices will be higherat each level of demand. If supply costs have not increased higher profits will be obtained; this will stimulate additional production until marginal costs and prices balance at a new level of supply. Similarly if demand decreases prices at each level of output will fall, profits will be reduced; eventually supply will fall until a new equilibrium is found.

Adjusting Capacity

The speed with which demand and supply adjust to each other depends on the nature of the industry. A market selling perishable goods has a supply fixed for that day and tends to adjust prices to clear the supply. From one day to another it can often change the level of supply in relation to the previous days demand but it may take a year or more to effect any large-scale change in supply. At one extreme supply may be more or less fixed, for example, old masters, while at the other supply may be flexible, for example, unskilled labour which can find employment in many different fields. Skilled and professional labour in building tends to take a long time to train, most plants for winning and producing building materials take several years to develop, so that while small building firms can be formed quite rapidly, it tends to take a long time to create new capacity once the industry has been run-down.

Of course, the construction industry does not produce a uniform product. Resources can be switched within limits from one type of output to another, from building to civil engineering and from new to maintenance work. Often however, demand changes in a similar direction for all the products of the industry and changes in demand cannot be cushioned by changing the mix of services provided.[①] Producing for stock has limited relevance in this industry partly because much of the work arises on customer's site and to his instructions and partly because the cost of the carrying stock, speculative building, is very expensive except when rates of interest are very low.

Notes

①然而，对所有工业品的需求常常在一个类似的方向上变化，而这种需求上的变化不能通过改变所提供的综合性服务来缓和。

UNIT FOUR

Text   Cash Forecast

[1]   To make a cash forecast it is necessary to estimate, usually by months, the times when progress payments may be expected and when any cash from other sources will be available. At this point a forecast of the statement of changes in financial position sometimes proves useful. In making a cash forecast it is necessary to anticipate the cash requirements of known work, overhead, taxes, equipment purchases, and loan repayments.

[2]   There are contractors who maintain that such forcasts are a waste of time because they become obsolete before they are prepared, due to the fact that the collectibility of payments is not predictable, and because they mislead the reader by anticipating funds not actually on hand. All these objections miss the point. The type of cash forecast accomplishes two things: (1) it inventories cash resources and balances expected needs against them; (2) it schedules the work that must be done and the collections that must be made if money is to be on hand to pay the bills.

[3]   Such cash forecasts, as used by progressive construction companies, are made quickly, because they do not seek to achieve more than approximate accuracy. However, they must be made by someone who knows conditions and who recognizes the forecasts for what they are— a financial plan to be followed as nearly as possible and to be updated as necessary. On the basis of such a forecast it is possible to estimate what short-term loans will be needed and how and when they will be repaid. With this type of forecast to show the banker, it will be easier for a deserving borrower to get the needed credit. If there is reason to believe that the collection of the expected funds will be slow, the forecast will call attention to the need for greater collection effort.

[4]   The expected availability of cash may make a great deal of difference in the way new work is estimated. If adequate working capital will be available, the contractor may bid more lump sum work. If working capital is likely to be tied up for some time, he may try to convert some of his lump sum bids to reimbursable cost-plus fee jobs financed by a client-furnished revolving fund. If work is scarce and jobs in progress are approaching completion, he might bid more competitively and on a lower margin in anticipation of being able to finance the work with funds from jobs closing out.①

[5]   Some cash forecasts are based on types of work rather than on individual jobs. Thus the captions for receipts might be something like "Contract work," "Maintenance work," "Repair jobs," and so on, and for expenditures, such items as "Payrolls", "Purchases", and "Taxes." In some types of construction businesses this is the only practical way.

[6]   There are three important limitations to the use of such a forecast. First, it is no more accurate than the thinking that goes into it.② Therefore it is not a mere juggling of figures to

be assigned to anyone who has nothing better to do. It is a monthly review of the immediate past and the best estimate of the course of the business for the immediate future. When it is being prepared, the best combined thinking of management together with its outside accountants and financial advisers is brought to bear on the immediate financial problems of the company. If the cash forecast is not prepared in this way it loses much of the meaning it should have, and may, in fact, become as misleading as its critics charge.

[7] Second, it must be remembered that a forecast guarantees nothing. The money expected will arrive only if the thinking that accompanied the forecast is translated into effective action. There is a strong temptation, particularly when a bank loan is being sought, to indulge in wishful thinking and overly optimistic guessing. This may work once but if the figures do not prove to be reasonable, the banker will tend to doubt all the contractor's estimates in the future. This could be disastrous to credit, and since the banks and bonding companies usually work very closely together it might well hurt the contractor's bonding capacity. Cash forecasting requires the same hardheaded realism as bidding. Excessive optimism in either can lead to serious trouble. On the other hand, careful, conservative forecasting can be one of the most useful tools of financial management.

[8] Third, a cash forecast is not necessarily indicative of profit or loss. A contractor may have a great deal of highly profitable work in process and still be very short of cash. In fact, he is often in that position. An expanding business works its money very hard, and working funds do not stay any longer in the bank account than working equipment stays in the contractor's yard. For purposes of tax planning and the long-range planning of operations, the proper procedure is to employ the "profit-and-loss" or "operations" forecast.

New Words and Expressions

progress payment		施工分期付款
statement of changes in financial position		资金变动情况表，财务状况变动表
anticipate [æn'tisipeit]	v.	预测
overhead ['əuvəhed]	n.	企业一般管理费，（商业）间接费用
repayment [ri:'peimənt]	n.	偿还；偿付的款项
obsolete * ['ɔbsəli:t]	a.	过时的，陈腐的，已不用的
collectibility [kəlekti'biliti]	n.	收集，征收，可收集性
predictable * [pri'diktəbl]	a.	可预报的，可预言的
inventory * ['invntri]	v.	为……编制目录，开列存货清单
collection [kə'lekʃən]	n.	收款，收帐，收入款项
update * [ʌp'deit]	v.	使现代化
repay [ri:'pei]	v.	偿还，还（钱等）
banker ['bæŋkə]	n.	银行家
borrower ['bɔrəuə]	n.	借贷者

bid *	[bid]	v.; n.	投标，出价
lump sum work			总额包干工作，金额一次总付的工作
tie up			冻结，（资金）搁置，（使资金等）专做某用金而不能随便使用
revolving fund			周转资金
reimbursable	[ˌriːmˈbɑːsəbl]	a.	补偿的，偿还的
cost-plus fee			成本加成费用
margin	[ˈmɑːdʒin]	n.	盈利，毛利；押金，保证金
caption	[ˈkæpʃən]	n.	（文件，文章等）标题，（图片等）解说词
expenditure *	[iksˈpenditʃə]	n.	支出，支出额，消费额
payroll	[ˈpeirəul]	n.	工资单，工资额
juggle	[ˈdʒʌgl]	v.	玩把戏，耍花招
accountant	[əˈkautənt]	n.	会计
adviser	[ədˈvaizə]	n.	顾问
misleading	[misˈliːdiŋ]	a.	引入歧途的；使人误解的
indulge (in)	[inˈdʌldʒ]	v.	沉迷，沉溺
wishful	[ˈwiʃful]	a.	怀有希望的，表示愿望的
overly	[ˈəuvəli]	ad.	过度地，过分地
disastrous	[diˈzɑːstrəs]	a.	造成惨重损失的，灾难性的
bonding company			担保公司
hardheaded	[ˈhɑːdˈhedid]	a.	冷静的，精明而讲实际的
realism	[ˈriəlisəm]	n.	（对人对事等）现实主义态度
indicative *	[inˈdikətiv]	a.	指示的，预示的
profitable *	[ˈprɔfitəbl]	a.	有益的，有利可图的

Notes

①主句中 more competitively，on a lower margin 和 in anticipating of ... out 都是 bid 的状语。

②句中 the thinking that goes into it 意为 "所认为，所想的。" 句中的两个 it 指代 forecast。

Exercises

Reading Comprehension

Ⅰ．Choose the best answer：

1. What is necessary to do in order to make a satisfactory cash forecast?

    A. To estimate the time when progress payment may be expected.
    B. To anticipate the cash equirements of known work, taxes, equipment purchases, etc.
    C. To estimate the time when any cash from other sources will be available.
    D. All of the above.
 2. Which statement is not true of some contractors mentioned in the text?
    A. They believe that cash forecasts become obsolete before they are prepared.
    B. They believe that cash forecasts are of no use since the collectibility of payments is not predictable.
    C. They believe that cash forecasts are useless because they balance expected needs against cash resources.
    D. They believe that cash forecasts mislead the reader by anticipating funds not actually on hand.
 3. Which is not true of "this type of forecast" in the sentence "with this type of forecast to show the banker, it will be easier for a deserving borrower to get the needed credit"?
    A. The forecast is made quickly.
    B. The forecast is made accurately.
    C. The forecast is made by someone who knows conditions.
    D. The forecast is made by someone who recognizes what the forecast is for.
 4. Even if on the basis of a useful forecast it is almost impossible for a construction company to estimate _____.
    A. what short-term loans will be needed
    B. when short-term loans will be needed
    C. how short-term loans will be repaid
    D. when short-term loans will be repaid
 5. A contractor may bid more competitively _____.
    A. if adequate working capital will be available
    B. if working capital is likely to be tied up for some time
    C. if work is scarce
    D. if jobs in progress are finishing

II. Match the five main features of forecast in Column A with their corresponding numbers of paragraphs where they exist in Column B.

A	B
1. A forecast used by progressive construction company is made quickly.	a. para. [7]
2. A forecast is based on types of work rather than on individual jobs.	b. para. [3]
3. A forecast is no more accurate than the thinking that goes into it.	c. para. [8]

4. A forecast guarantees nothing.   d. para. [6]
5. A forecast is not necessarily indicative of profit or loss.   e. para. [5]

Vocabulary

I. Fill in the blanks with the words given below. Change the form if necessary.

> indicative,   anticipate,   caption,   guarantee,   limitation

1. Do not _____ your earnings by spending a lot of money.
2. He gave the bank the papers which proved his ownership of the house as a _____ that he would repay the money provided by the bank.
3. His high forehead is _____ of great mental power.
4. This problem will not be dealt with at the meeting owing to the _____ of time.
5. I read no further than the _____ because the subject of the article seemed uninteresting.

II. Match the words in Column A with their corresponding definitions in Column B.

A	B
1. profitable	a. careful, kept with reasonable limits
2. obsolete	b. out of date, no longer used
3. overhead	c. too much
4. conservative	d. resulting in money gain
5. overly	e. money spent regularly to keep a business running

Reading Material A

Profit-and-loss Forecast

The forecast of profit and loss is not commonly used by smaller contractors because it is based, essentially, on the concept of break-even point. In manufacturing and marketing the break-even point is that volume of sales which will produce enough gross profit to pay the fixed overhead expenses. In construction, the volume of job revenue tends to vary more and to be subject to greater fluctuations in the rate of gross profit than the sales of a manufacturing or marketing business.① The concept is, therefore, harder to apply to construction. One notable exception is the builder of tract housing whose operations, in many respects, are similar to those of a manufacturer. Another such exception is the plumber or electrician who does a large volume of small maintenance jobs. These operations are similar to a retail marketing business.

31

For the most part, however, construction companies tend to have less predictable fluctuations both in volume of business done and in gross profit.

Nevertheless, in a market where there is a reasonable amount of available business, and assuming a reasonable degree of skill in estimating, the principal factors limiting the volume of a contractor's business are the amount of his capital and the size and ability of his organization. If recognition is given to these two factors, a contractor may, by comparing the results of past operations with a sound estimate of present and future conditions, arrive at a reasonable estimate of the volume of work which he can reasonably expect to complete and the average gross profit which he can reasonably expect that amount of work to produce.② In fact, some contractors start their profit-and-loss forecasting with an estimate of expected annual gross profit. Others estimate gross profit in terms of a stated number of dollars per permanent employee.

To illustrate a somewhat more conventional approach, assume a building contractor finds that over the past several years he has been able to earn net job revenue (gross profit) averaging 6 percent on total job revenue (contract price of completed work). Assume further that his estimate of the market for the coming year combined with the capacity of his organization and the amount of available working capital lead him to believe that he can complete $3 million in contract volume and make an average of 6 percent gross profit on it. On the basis of these assumptions, the contractor must keep his overhead under $18 000 if he is to make a profit.

This sort of planning requires a very high degree of management skill and usually the best of outside advice. Once the technique is mastered, however, it enables the contractor to use his available resources to the greatest possible extent and to the greatest possible advantage. To make such estimates the first requirement is accurate financial statemints prepared on a consistent basis over a period of several years. The second, and equally important requirement, is a record of past forecasts and the amounts and reasons for their variations from actual operating results. The third requirement is a sound analysis of existing and future market conditions coupled with sound planning for making the most of them. Combining these three elements, a sound and conservative management can forecast operating results with a high degree of accuracy and in so doing can develop the information necessary to plan the most effective use of its organization, equipment, and capital.

Notes

① 在建筑行业中，工程收入总额比制造业和销售业的销售额变化更频繁、更容易导致毛利的大幅波动。
② 如果认识到这两个因素，承包商可以通过把过去经营结果同目前及未来形势的正确估算相比较的方法，得到一个对他预期能够完成的工作总量和他预期的这种工作量所能够带来的平均毛利润的合理估算。

Reading Material B

Reporting

The reason for the limited usefulness of the basic records is the fact that they are not necessarily designed to make significant groupings or comparisons. That is the function of reporting—in other words, the financial statements. The mere statement that a construction company has $ 25 000 in cash means very little by itself. However, if it is stated that the company has $ 25 000 cash and $ 150 000 in current receivables and other current assets, and that its current liabilities total $ 100 000, the figures begin to be significant.

To the person in charge of credit at the lumber yard this would normally mean that the company is in a position to pay its bills currently and that, other things being equal, a reasonable line of credit is probably justified. To the banker and to the bonding company, it would indicate the probability that the company could be reasonably expected to handle a backlog of work of, say, $ 750 000 to $ 1 000 000, without getting into financial difficulties. To the contractor himself it would indicate that if he has much less than $ 750 000 backlog his money is not working as hard as it should be, and if he has much more than $ 1 000 000 backlog he may be overextending himself.

Naturally the significance of the amounts involved will vary with all the circumstances and will not depend solely on current position. It is for the financial statements to bring out all the significant facts essential to a proper evaluation of the company's current financial position and the results of its operations. [1]

Suppose, however, that the company referred to above were a subcontractor working on lump sum contracts, and that included in $ 150 000 of current receivables were $ 100 000 in retained percentages due from prime contractors. If the subcontractor could not expect to be paid for these retentions until the prime contractors were paid their retentions by the owners, then the subcontractor's funds could be partially frozen, so that he might have only $ 50 000 in net working capital available. Naturally, the volume of work that he might take on successfully would be reduced proportionately. On the other hand, the volume of work that the contractor could undertake would not be greatly affected if all his contracts were on a cost-plus-fixed-fee basis using owner-furnished revolving funds.

It is the function of the balance sheet to give, as well as possible, a fair summary of the assets, liabilities, and net worth of the business at a given time. It is the function of the operating statement to give a fair summary of the results of operations during a given period.

Notes

①摆出所有的对公司财政现状以及公司经营结果的合理评估必不可少的重要因素是为了做好财务报表。

UNIT FIVE

Text   The Successful Proposal

[1]   The successful proposal was submitted generally in accordance with established methods. In this example, the owner also requested proposals from two local general contractors. After evaluating the proposals, the owner chose the professional construction management approach as being best suited to the requirements of this particular project.

[2]   A summary of the successful construction management (CM) proposal is set forth on the following pages. The proposal consists of a letter that outlines proposed services and quotes a fixed fee for home office services, general overhead, and profit.

CM PROPOSAL

Easyway Dry Storage Warehouse

CONSTRUCTION MANAGEMENT & CONTROL, INC.

September 1, 1984

Proposal No. 84-17

Mr. Peter · J · Cleaveland

Manager, Design & Construction Department

Easyway Food Company

200 Madison Street

Mountaintown, WestAmerica 99999

Subject: Professional Construction Management Proposal

           Mountaintown Dry Storage Warehouse

Dear Mr. Cleaveland:

[3]   In accordance with your request we are pleased to submit this proposal to furnish Professional Construction Management services for construction of the Mountaintown Dry Storage Warehouse.

[4]   Construction Management & Control, Inc. proposes to provide a management services program structured to meet the objective of achieving the benefits of fixed-price construction.[①] Through use of the "Fast Track" (or phased construction) approach, fixed-price construction contracts will be developed, bid, and awarded to permit building closure at the earliest possible date. This will enable interior work to continue during the winter months in order to permit owner occupancy on schedule next spring.

[5]   We propose herein that Construction Management & Control, Inc. will provide the following services:

[6]   1 *Prepare Control Schedule*   Prepare a master control schedule showing the contemplated bid packages and the required construction duration for achieving project objectives.

[7]   2 *Develop Bid Packages*   With the assistance of owner and architect, develop a de-

35

tailed scope of the separate bid packages applicable for lumpsum bidding. ②

[8] 3 *Prepare Bidders List* Handle prequalification of prospective bidders having the specialized skills necessary for accomplishing the work. A bid list will be prepared in consultation with architect and owner.

[9] 4 *Prepare Fair-Cost Estimates* A fair-cost estimate for each bid pack-age will be prepared for use in evaluating bids.

[10] 5 *Receive, Review, and Evaluate Bids* Bid openings will be conducted. bids evaluated, and recommendations prepared for contract award by Easyway Food Company. Inc. ③

[11] 6 *Manage, Coordinate, and Inspect the Work* It is our understanding that a representative of Easyway Food Company. Inc. will visit the work periodically, and that the architect will also make periodic visits as required. Construction Management & Control, Inc. will provide a full-time Field Construction Manager who will be assigned to the site for managing, coordinating, and inspecting all work performed on the project. His duties will include coordination of contracts; monitoring the schedule of individual phases of the work; making recommendations for adjusting the work to accommodate changing and unforeseen conditions if applicable; preparation of reports on the progress of the work; reviewing and recommending progress payments; obtaining required shop drawings and forwarding them to the architect for approval; obtaining testing laboratory services as required; inspecting the quality of materials and workmanship; maintaining daily logs and records; and such other services as are customarily required in order to manage the work in accordance with the owner's objectives. ④

[12] 7 *Provide Home-Office Support Services* Construction Management & Control, Inc. will designate one individual in the office who will be responsible to the owner's Project Manager for all work, and who will be utilized on an "as required" basis to the extent necessary for this purpose. In addition the resources of Construction Management & Control, Inc. 's management and technical personnel will be available for assistance to the owner throughout the project in the event of special need.

[13] We propose to provide the Professional Construction Management services for a fixed fee to cover home office services, with all field costs to be reimbursable. ⑤ Our fixed fee will be One Hundred Thousand Dollars ($ 100 000. 00).

[14] Our proposal is subject to the negotiation of a mutually satisfactory agreement.

[15] We greatly appreciate the opportunity to provide our proposal for Professional Construction Management services for your Mountaintown project. Since our proposal has been developed on the basis of preliminary information, we would be pleased to discuss the program further, and incorporate modifications if required, in order to more fully comply with your overall objectives.

                              Very truly yours,
                              CONSTRUCTION MANAGEMENT & CONTROL, INC.

JWH: mp   J. Walter Harrington
Attach.   President

New Words and Expressions

set forth			宣布；发表
warehouse *	['wɛəhaus]	n.	货栈，仓库
completion *	[kəm'pli:ʃən]	n.	完成，结束
bid *	[bid]	v.	投标；出价
closure *	['kləuʒə]	n.	截止；关闭
occupancy *	['ɔkjupənsi]	n.	（土地，房屋等之）占有，占用
herein *	['hiərin]	ad.	在此处，此中
contemplate	['kɔntempleit]	v.	打算；考虑
architect *	['ɑ:kitekt]	n.	建筑师
lump-sum	['lʌmp'sʌm]	a.	一次总付的
bidder	['bidə]	n.	投标人；出价人
prequalification	[pri(:)ˌkwɔlifi'keiʃən]	n.	事先审查
prospective *	[prəs'pektiv]	a.	有希望的；预期的
consultation	[kɔnsʌl'teiʃən]	n.	商议；参考
periodically	[ˌpiəri'ɔdikəli]	ad.	定期的；周期地
periodic	[ˌpiəri'ɔdik]	a.	定期的；周期的
unforeseen	['ʌnfɔ:'si:n]	a.	预料不到的；事先不知道的
forward	['fɔ:wəd]	vt.	转送；发送
workmanship	['wə:kmənʃip]	n.	手艺；技艺，工作质量
log	[lɔg]	n.	（工作，航行）记录
customarily	['kʌstəmrili]	ad.	通常；习惯上
designate *	['dezigneit]	vt.	指定，选派
negotiation	[niɡəuʃi'eiʃən]	n.	协商；谈判
mutually	['mju:tjuəli]	ad.	相互地；彼此地
modification *	[mɔdifi'keiʃən]	n.	修改；改进
comply	[kəm'plai]	vi.	（与 with 连用）遵守；照做

Notes

①... structured to ... construction contracts：过去分词短语作后置定语，修饰 program；短语中 while preserving … contracts 作短语的状语从句。

②a scope of ... 相当于 a range of ... , a series of ... , 意思是 "一系列的"。

③此句是个并列句,... bids evaluated, and recommendations prepared for … 中省略了 "will be "。

④此句的宾语很长，共有十个直到此段结束。accommodate：译作 "顺应，适应"；progress

37

payments：施工分期付款。

⑤ ... with all field costs to be reimbursable：介词短语作条件状语。

Exercises

Reading Comprehension

Ⅰ. Choose the best answer.

1. The successful Construction Management (CM) proposal is generally composed by _____.

    A. a letter

    B. the outline of proposed services and estimates of construction management costs

    C. the evaluation of the proposal

    D. the back ground of the bidding company

2. The management services program of Construction Management & Control, Inc. is mainly intended to _____.

    A. permit the owner to occupy the new warehouse at the earliest possible date

    B. preserve the benefits of Construction Management & Control, Inc.

    C. ensure the warehouse will be completed on schedule in ten months

    D. save construction management costs

3. Construction Management & Control, Inc. will be responsible for _____.

    A. conducting the bidding process of construction contracts

    B. constructing the warehouse

    C. developing the owner's objectives

    D. None of the above

4. If unforeseen conditions emerge, the Field Construction Manager should _____.

    A. take actions promptly to adjust the work

    B. report on the conditions to both companies

    C. recommending alternative adjusting actions

    D. both B and C

5. Construction Management & Control, Inc. appoints one individual in the home office to _____.

    A. act as Project Manager

    B. function just on the basis of "required"

    C. assist the Project Manager for all work performed on the project

    D. prepare the report on the resources of its management and technical personnel

Ⅱ. Say whether the following statements are True (T) or False (F) according to the text.

(   ) 1. The time-span of construction completion is stated in the master control schedule.

(   ) 2. The prequalification of prospective bidders is conducted by Easyway Food Company Inc.

( ) 3. Construction Management & Control Inc will give some advice on which bid of construction contract is more suitable for the project.

( ) 4. A Field Construction Manager will be assigned to the construction site for managing, coordinating and inspecting all work and therefore, Easyway Food Company doesn't need to be involved in the construction of the project.

( ) 5. The total construction management cost including all field costs will be $ 100 000 00.

Vocabulary

I. Fill in the blanks with the words given below. Change the form if necessary.

> reimbursable, prequalification, bidder,
> bid, modification, prospective, designate

1. A few construction companies are _____ for the contract to build the bridge.
2. The manager will single out one person from the _____ applicants as his assistant.
3. Before Mary was to go on a business trip her boss promised that all the travelling expenses would be _____.
4. Just several _____ to this plan will greatly improve it.
5. Mr. Wyman has been _____ to take over the position of party chairman.

II. Match the words in Column A with their corresponding definitions in Column B.

A	B
1. lump-sum	a. to make changes that take account of wishes or demands of sb. or sth.
2. contemplate	b. an officially written record of a journey esp. in a ship or a plan
3. accommodate	c. (an amount of money) given or received as a single unit rather than in separate parts at different times.
4. log	d. the act of talking with another person or group in order to try to come to an agreement
5. negotiation	e. to think deeply or thoughtfully

Reading Material A

Insurance

There are many risks and liabilities that concern the architect or engineer in the construction of a project. The AIA and the EJCDC general conditions each deal with basic insurance requirements, but neither includes amounts of coverage or other types of insurance coverage that may be necessary to safeguard the interests of all parties to the contract, including the designers. ① Obviously, the contractor bears most of the responsibility, but the owner and the designer may have contingent liability. ② To safeguard them, their names may be added to some insurance policies as additional insured parties.

The general conditions should be modified by means of supplementary conditions to include the policy limits that the contractor will be required to furnish. ③ These limits vary somewhat with the size and character of the project, with its location, and with the risks involved. However, it is not correct that a $1 million project should carry one-twentieth the insurance coverage that a $20 million project carries. Keep in mind that an accident is an accident, whether the project is large or small. The award for a lost limb will be no lower on the $1 million project. For this reason the coverage limits may be remarkably alike on small and large projects. The big differences may lie in the number of types of insurance coverage, as will be determined by the owner, his attorney, and his insurance advisor according to nature of the work and its risks.

In order to be sure that the insurance that has been specified is in effect on the project, the owner, with the help of the architect, must require that a certificate of insurance listing all pertinent insurance facts be furnished by the contractor's insurance company. ④ Since each insurance company may issue its own form of certificate, it is often difficult to understand readily what is actually stated in a certificate.

To ensure speedy and thorough evaluation of insurance, the AIA has prepared a Certificate of Insurance form which provides for the description of each policy type or risk covered, the listing of policy numbers, inception and expiration dates, and for the limits of liability under each category. ⑤ This form reveals more than does the commonly used Acord form, favored by many insurance agents. Entries in the Acord form are frequently abbreviated or coded in such a way that persons unfamiliar with insurance will have difficulty an alyzing the information.

The AIA, through its Committee on Insurance, has developed another standard form, Owner's Instructions for Bonds and Insurance to help the architect to obtain and record the owner's wishes in these matters. It is important that the specifier or project manager put this questionnaire in the hands of the owner, with an appropriate cover letter, before the preparation of contract documents begins. Owners do not always respond to this request for information, even after calls from the specifier. If an owner delays returning his instructions beyond the project manual print date, the specifier has no choice but to leave the specifics of insurance and bonding out of the supplementary conditions. It would be unwise to make decisions of this kind for an owner—in fact most carriers of professional liability insurance specifically exclude the architect from coverage if he ventures into the area of making judgments about the insurance for a project.⑥ It is probably safe for the specifier, after checking with his firm's attorney, to include a provision such as this in the supplementary conditions after giving the owner timely notice of his intent: "The extent and cost of insurance coverage shall be negotiated by the Owner and apparent successful bidder before award of contract and execution of the Agreement."

Notes

①美国建筑师协会和哥伦比亚特区工程师联合委员会的普通保险条款都只涉及基本的保险要求,两者并没有将保险总额和其它种类的保险险别包括在内,而这些对于维护合同内的所有团体(包括设计师)的利益来说也许是很必要的。
②contingent liability:意外责任。
③policy limits:保险范围。
④为了确保已指定的保险在工程有效,业主必须在建筑师的帮助下要求承包人的保险公司提供一份列有所有相关的保险事实的保险证书。
⑤inception and expiration dates:起始与终止日期
⑥对于业主来说做出此种决定将是不明智的。如果他敢于对工程投保做些判断就会发现事实上绝大多数职业责任保险的承保人都特意将建筑师排除在保险范围之外。

Reading Material B

Selecting a Method of Computerized Specifying

The range of available hardware, from dedicated word processor through PC and mainframe computer, increases the number of options that a design office has in producing its specifications.

The method that will be selected for specification production varies according to the vast range of different office types and conditions of practice.

1. Notes on the Drawings. Sometimes the architect or engineer is contracted to do drawings only. The notes and certain information required by public authorities are the only gesture in the direction of specifications.①

2. Specifications on the Drawings. Actually a very effective method, calling forth the best

in concise writing. Unfortunately, this method is usually very poorly executed, partly because formats have not been developed to ease this mode of production, and partly because of the low fee that forced the designer to take this shortcut in the first place.

3. Pro Forma Specifications. The method often resorted to when fee is slim or time is short.[2] An old specification or text for another project is duplicated at high speed, with little editing, to give the appearance of a specification effort.[3] This is the lowest level at which computerized methods help much.

4. Condensed Specifications. Excellent work has been done in short-form specifications, whether for reproduction with the drawings or for issue in a slim book.[4] There is a move in the profession toward this type of specification production. When information is efficiently compressed, not abbreviated, specifying can be effective and can meet the standard of professional care expected by the courts.

5. Knowledge-Based Specifications. Especially effective in the small office without a specifier, but also used in larger firms to cut research and editing time. Whether or not the office has a PC, this method can be used to produce professionally prepared text by computer, in house or remote.

6. Consultant Specifications. Another option for the office without sufficient specification writing resources. Many consultants are in practice fulltime, maintain libraries, and are available during working hours. Most consultants use efficient computer systems and have developed master texts that dovetail with local needs.

7. Consultant-Prepared Master. In this mode of specification production the skilled work of preparing and periodically updating a master is done by the consultant. Editing is done in house by job captains or a specification editor.[5] Usually, the consultant is retained to handle problems as they come up, on an hourly fee basis.

8. Nationally Available Master Specification. By using one of the well developed master text systems, The specifier can draw on sections written and coordinated to the level of competence expected of architects and engineers.[6] Editing is required, followed by processing in the office or by sending out to service bureaus that provide fast turnaround time for specifications.

9. Office Master Specification. A master can be developed in the office by an office specification staff, or a commercial master can be adapted to the office's needs. Editing can be done by the same staff, or, as is common in many larger offices, by each studio or project team.

10. Integrated System. In highly computerized offices links are being made between drawings and specifications. Code and product and cost databases are being used, and beneficial information such as quantities and cost analysis is being generated along with contract documents. Where this is the case, the responsibility is usually centered in one or a few individuals who are aware of the desired end product: the design intent. High-quality documents can result as this process is perfected in use. As these integrated systems develop to the level at which decisions and information in one part of the system cause information in other parts to change or response to take place, the level of true expert systems is reached.[7]

Notes

①政府当局需要的记录和某些信息是文本输出时唯一的方向性暗示。
②当经费不足或时间不多时,此方法常常被采用。
③快速地复制一份为另一项工程所做的旧文本,几乎不经过什么编辑,却能让人感觉是费了心力才做出的一份文本。
④Issue in a slim book:制作一本薄册子。
⑤job captains:汇编程序员。
⑥通过利用一种发展得十分完善的主文本系统,文本制作人可利用分部说明然后将分部说明与建筑师和工程师预期应达到的竞争力水平协调起来(的方法设计文本)。
⑦当这些综合系统发展到系统内一部分的决策和信息能引起另一些部分的信息进行改变或引起另一些部分发生反应的这种水平时,真正的专家系统的水平也具有了。

UNIT SIX

Text   Architecture Is a Volatile Business

Crises

[1]   No business stands still or does not have crises. Crises usually come from external events which are outside the partners' control. All you can do is to react and take action to mitigate loss or perhaps achieve a gain from the situation facing you.

[2]   Crises which occur internally are of a different nature. They can be the result of a long period of tension or disharmony which comes to a head as the 'last straw'.[①] Senior staff movements can cause major disruptions which affect the quality of your services.

[3]   In many ways these crises are minimal compared with the effects of national and international booms and slumps. How do these affect practice?

[4]   Let us now look at the characteristics of booms, slumps and transitions from slump to boom and boom to slump.

Slump

[5]   There have been two recognisable slumps during this century: the late 1920s and early 30s, and the middle 1970s into the early 1980s. Cuts in government expenditure, particularly those affecting capital projects, have been responsible for slumps in the building industry, and consequent loss of work for architects. The effect starts with changes in the stock market and interest rates, lower customer expenditure leading to shut downs of factories and large pockets of unemployment.[②] The first reaction is to cut down on capital expenditure which is the life blood of our business.

Boom

[6]   The most notable boom in the last twenty years was from 1970-3 when the government thought it could increase prosperity by increasing money supply and encouraging private enterprise.

[7]   Booms are normally noticed after they have actually occurred. Everyone experiences an increase in activity. Offices start to get more work and want to expand. This is a period of security, excitement, confidence and achievement but by the nature of our society booms do not last for very long.[③]

Transition from Boom to Slump

[8]   This transition can be the most painful and it requires the greatest skill to manage.

[9]   Obviously the first signs of transition mean that the workload decreases and staff have to be dismissed. It is always a painful and difficult process. Problems related to premises, sudden downturns in cash flow, superfluous equipment and restructuring of the whole business are all parts of this process. ④ Often at the end of a boom there is an overrun when there are a considerable number of projects on site and cash is still flowing in, but there is a noticeable diminution of projects coming into the office.

[10]   The cash is still being spent to meet the extra work created during the boom and yet the signs are ominous and cutbacks have to be planned. The most expensive element in any office is staff and this is the first task to be tackled. The decision whether to make old staff redundant and retain new bright staff is painful and very difficult as often directors and partners may differ from one another in their view of the effectiveness of the staff under them.

[11]   Cutting a lot of the extra facilities which could be afforded in a boom often has a noticeable effect on staff morale, particularly as premises shrink and everyone begins to work more closely together in new teams. Therefore, when this type of change has to take place and the office shrinks, people go, salaries level out, rises are less, work is more competitive, fees are lower, competition within the office itself is intense. ⑤ This requires probably the greatest management skills to weather the storm and come out intact, so that you can make profits in the midst of recession and be prepared for the upward transition which will inevitably come. ⑥

Transition from Slump to Boom

[12]   If you are coming out of recession and business is picking up, there is more workload, money is easier to borrow, you are operating from an optimistic economic base and people are not exhausted from overwork.

[13]   The first question when work increases is whether you have sufficient funds to finance the operation. You may go to see your bank manager for more finance in a period when most of his customers in general business are still in the depths of, or just recovering from the recession. ⑦ This means that you have to be very persuasive and confident that your forecasts are going to prove correct so that you can raise enough money to fund the new expansion. Perhaps the hardest task is to persuade your sources of finance that expenditure now is going to reap rewards in the future.

[14]   As expansion occurs you will need new premises. This often causes much difficulty and debate during a period when you want to concentrate your efforts on the new work coming in. The leasing, purchase and quipping of premises is very capital intensive and, at these

45

times, capital is often needed to fund the projects which are pouring into the office.⑧ As a result, even though work is pouring in, you will experience cash flow difficulties and will have to obtain medium term loans or arrange for monthly fee payments from clients, probably at slightly reduced fees overall in order to maintain liquidity during this period of expansion.⑨ You must also remember during this period that transitions leading to boom eventually result in booms leading to transitions, perhaps in turn leading to recession, and you may in a few years be back to the workload from which you started.

New Words and Expressions

mitigate ['mitigeit]	v.	缓和；减轻
disharmony [dis'hɑ:məni]	n.	不协调；不调和
disruption * [dis'rʌpʃən]	n.	分裂；瓦解；破裂
minimal * ['miniməl]	a.	最小的；最低的
boom * [bu:m]	n.	（市面的）忽然兴旺；繁荣；（形势的）突然好转
slump [slʌmp]	n.	经济萧条；消沉；[商]（事业的）衰败；低落
transition * [træn'ziʃən, træn'siʃən]	n.	过渡（时期）；转折
recognisable ['rekəgnaizəbl]	a.	可承认（公认）的；面熟的
expenditure * [iks'penditʃə]	n.	（金钱，时间等）支出，花费；费用
consequent ['kɔnsikwənt]	a.	随之发生的；因…而起的
notable * ['nəutəbl]	a.	显著的；值得注意的；著名的
enterprise * ['entəpraiz]	n.	企（事）业单位；兴办（企业）
workload ['wə:kləud]	n.	（规定期限的）工作量；工作负担
premise * ['premis]	n. (pl)	房屋（及其附属基地、建筑等）；前提；根据
downturn ['dauntə:n]	n.	下降趋势；下转
superfluous [sju:'pəfluəs]	a.	过多的；多余的
diminution [dimi'nju:ʃən]	n.	减少；减缩；缩小
ominous ['ɔminəs]	a.	不祥的，不吉；预兆的
cutback ['kʌtbæk]	n.	削减；中止
redundant * [ri'dʌndənt]	a.	过多的，过剩的；冗长的
effectiveness * [i'fektivnis]	n.	效率；有效性
morale [mɔ'rɑ:l]	n.	士气，精神；信心
level ['levl]	v.	使同等；拉平
competitive * [kəm'petitiv]	a.	竞争的；竞赛的
weather ['weðə]	v.	[海]战胜（渡过）暴风雨；(喻) 渡过

intact *	[in'tækt]	a.	未受损的；完整无损的
recession	[ri'seʃən]	n.	（工商业的）衰退；（价格的）暴跌
overwork	['əuvəwəːk]	n.	繁重工作；过渡劳累
persuasive	[pə'sweisiv]	a.	有说服本领的，嘴巧的
lease	[liːs]	v.	出租，租用
liquidity	[li'kwiditi]	n.	流畅，流动性

Notes

①come to a head：（时机，事件等）成熟，逼近紧要关头；此处指不利的情况发展到了顶点，到了必须解决的时候。the last straw 指一系列打击下终于使人不能忍受的最后一击或最后因素。

②shut downs of factories 中的 shut downs 是由与其相应的动词词组变化而成的名词，译为"停业，关闭"。pockets of unemployment 失业区。

③by the nature of... 就... 本质而言。

④related to premises 为分词短语，作后置定语，修饰 problems。

⑤level out 与 level off 同义，"拉平，达到一定水平"，或指事态，事物保持稳定，水平。

⑥come out 有"结果是，显现"之意，形容词 intact 作表语。

⑦in the depths of 与 from 共用宾语 recession；in the depths of 译为"在... 正中，在... 的深处"。

⑧capital intensive：资本大量投资的。

⑨probably at slightly reduced fees overall... 中的 overall 为副词，相当于 on the whole, generally 即"总体上，总的说来"，在句中作状语，slightly reduced 是分词作定语修饰 fees, at ... fees 以... 样的价格，费用。

Exercises

Reading Comprehension

I. Choose the best answer.

1. The slumps in the building industry are mainly caused by _____.

    A. cuts in government expenditure

    B. rapid changes in the stock market

    C. decrease in customers' purchasing power

    D. the diminution of workload

2. The first problem needed to be solved during the transition from boom to slump is _____.

    A. cutting the extra facilities

B. protecting the staff morale

C. adjusting the arrangement of staff

D. cutting down on capital expenditure

3. During the transition from boom to slump, _____.

   A. cash stops flowing in

   B. few projects can be acquired

   C. a large number of new bright staff will be employed

   D. the superfluous equipment is to be cut

4. According to the author, in the transition from slump to boom, _____.

   A. everything looks wonderful and business is easy to manage

   B. you will still experience some difficulties in business though the future is optimistic

   C. the condition is absolutely contrary to that from boom to slump

   D. you can run your business as you like

5. If you want to get more finance from your bank manager in a period of unfavorable business climate you should _____.

   A. show him your ability in running business and your previous achievement

   B. let him know that you are confident of your projects and persuade him to believe your forecasts are going to prove correct

   C. assure him that the investment now will get more profits in the future

   D. both B and C

II. Say whether the following statements are True (T) or False (F) according to the text.

(   ) 1. In slumps business men should manage to stimulate the customer expenditure which makes our business alive.

(   ) 2. In the early 70s money supply increased and private business became prosperous.

(   ) 3. It's difficult to make the decision whether to dismiss old staff and get new staff because the opinions of partners and directors on the effectiveness of the staff are different and it will probably break the harmonic relationship between them.

(   ) 4. During the transition from boom to slump, staff morale always becomes very low because the payment is not satisfactory and working condition is worse.

(   ) 5. The purpose of the author on writing the last paragraph is to warn the business men not to be too optimistic in favorable economic condition and make some preparation for bad condition which is inevitable.

Vocabulary

I. Fill in the blanks with the words given below. Change the form if necessary.

> premises, finance, superfluous, mitigate, disruption, lease, minimal

1. It's very difficult to _____ an office at a comparatively low price in booms.
2. You can open an account with a five-dollar _____ deposit.
3. Taxes on business _____ are higher than those on private buildings.
4. Since money is lacking, we can not afford so many _____ equipment we don't need much.
5. The company can not run any longer if the manager is unable to get some _____ from the bank.

II. Match the words in Column A with their corresponding definitions in Column B.

A	B
1. recession	a. following as a result
2. expenditure	b. no longer employed because there is not enough work
3. redundant	c. the state of becoming smaller
4. diminution	d. a period of reduced trade and business activity
5. consequent	e. spending

Reading Material A

Staff-effect of Booms and Slumps

Staff account for approximately 50 to 70 per cent of the total expenses of an architect's office. It is this area where, in a period of recession, the biggest savings can be made. How do we set about such a task? First a list of staff should be prepared, showing for each individual their qualifications, duties, current projects and the time span of those projects, their salaries and length of service, and details of their personal background.

Then the workload has to be studied, with a reasonable forecast of future projects, and a structure drawn up relating to the realities of what the office will be doing over the next year. This in turn must be related to the expected cash flow over that period. This should identify any shortfall in cash which would have to be met by reduction in staff or premises. ①

When the new structure has been drawn up and staff costs checked to meet the cash targets, then the most difficult task is to assess each individual. Each staff member should be assessed in terms of ability, performance, potential for development, the possession of special skills and personal behaviour, e. g. appearance and punctuality. ② When this assessment has been carried out, then comes the difficult moment when the choice has to be made by the principals as to who stays and who will fit into the new structure. ③

The overall principle must be that the people chosen to remain in the structure must in the end make up a balanced and effective team. This is the most difficult of all management decisions.

Administrative staff present a more difficult problem because it is often less easy to measure performance. Some administrative staff occupy key positions and you cannot afford to lose them even though their workload may reduce because of the recession.

One of the first tasks is to look at the ratio of administrative staff to technical staff. If the ratio in your office is between 1∶3 and 1∶5 and you feel the staff are fully employed, then you probably have the right balance. If it is less or more then there may be some serious problem ahead.

During periods of boom, secretaries often get salary increases until their salaries are well above the market level, but are doing a job which could be done by someone at a much lower salary level. Is the higher paid but experienced secretary more valuable than someone less experienced or loyal? In a period of recession it may be the best policy to have expensive secretaries doing more jobs effectively and efficiently than to have younger, less experienced people who may be cheaper to employ. However, if cash is the most important problem, the sacrifice may have to be made and the expensive secretaries must go.

The other problem that may affect reduction in staff is when the firm is multi-disciplinary and has engineers and quantity surveyors within the organisation. It is well known that engineers and quantity surveyors need more projects to keep the same site team busy than architects. Therefore when a reduction in work comes, the quantity surveying and engineering sections may well have to take bigger cuts than the architects'. The problem then is whether there are enough people left to provide the same service which was probably originally set up during a boom period.

The main criterion should be establishing a realistic structure for the current circumstances.

In periods of expansion it is often necessary to expand the number of engineering and quantity surveying staff at a greater rate than the architects. This could lead to an imbalance in the type of services offered. The balance of disciplines in an office must be carefully monitored to see that the overall objective of the office in providing a multi-disciplinary service is maintained so that the office does not acquire a reputation of being predominantly one discipline.④

Notes

①资金的短缺会导致裁员或办公室的缩小。
②be assessed in terms of …在…方面给予评价。
③主句为一个倒装句,主语后紧跟着一个定语从句,译为:随之而来的便是该由负责人们决定谁最后留下来组成一个平衡而有效的队伍,这是所有管理决策中最难决策的。
④必须十分注意一个办公室中工作人员的专业结构的平衡,以保证办公室的提供多种专业服务的总目标不变,这样才不致于让办公室背上主要只有一个专业的名声。

Reading Material B

Professional Indemnity Insurance[①]

Professional indemnity (or PI) insurance is so specialised that there are only a few brokers who are expert in it. It is therefore best to get quotations from all of them and use these to negotiate the best deal for yourself. Every year when renewals are made you should check the market again to see that you are getting a fair deal.

All policies have "excess" clauses which means that the insured bears a specified proportion of every claim.[②] If you decide to opt for a higher excess you may well be able to reduce the premium paid.[③]

PI policies also provide that the insured architect hands over the right to conduct all litigation to his insurers, who will process the case while you get on with running your business. Some claims arise from clients who are in financial difficulties, or who are even straight rogues, and who wish to avoid paying fees by counterclaiming for negligence and breach of professional duties.[④] If your insurer settles rather than fighting what may be a valid case this will probably go against your principles. But remember, litigation is costly in time and emotional energy.

Above all you should realise that, since most policies cover only claims made within the year of insurance, you will need to maintain a policy not only for the rest of your professional life, but also after you have retired, since although you can only be sued in contract six years from the date when the breach took place, in tort you can be sued in negligence up to six years from the time when the damage to a building occurs.[⑤]

There are a few basic rules that should be followed:

(1) Read the proposal form carefully. Get legal advice if you have any doubts about the legal interpretation of clauses.

(2) Fill in the proposal form carefully and truthfully.

(3) You must be certain of notifying your insurers of any potential claim, even one as trivial as a leaking roof. Otherwise the insurer can avoid the policy on the grounds of non-disclosure. Your duty is to disclose everything which would affect the mind of a prudent underwriter in granting or renewing a policy or in determining the premium.

(4) In choosing the amount of cover, work roughly on two to three times annual fee turnover.[⑥] This should cover small practices, though large practices will have to do more accurate assessments to get the right cover.

(5) Look carefully to ensure you know what is covered in your insurance. You will not normally be covered for reimbursement of costs in defence of a claim, unless you have additional legal expenses cover, although of course if you are successful in your defence you will get an

order for costs from the court.⑦

(6) Have a QC clause in case you need independent advice on how the defence to your claim should be conducted, as this may differ from your insurer's view.⑧

(7) If dealing with consultants, such as civil engineers or quantity surveyors, do not enter into direct contract with them but make sure that the employer engages them. You will then have no legal liability for them. You should advise the client to check that his other consultants are adequately insured.

(8) Make sure that your insurance covers retired partners and any past project carried out by the practice even before the current partners or directors were in charge.

You should realise that insurance companies, like any other business, need to make a profit each year. They will therefore seek to limit their losses and will apply well tried methods to mitigate claims.

Notes

①professional indemnity insurance：职业保障保险。
②所有的保险单都有附加条款，它们意味着被保险人（受保户）将承受每一索赔的指定部分。
③opt for：选择 premium：保险费。
④rogues：无赖. by counterclaiming for negligence and breach of professional duties：通过反诉（建筑设计师）玩忽职守。
⑤be sued：被起诉，被控告。
    in tort：民事侵权行为（不包括违背契约）。
⑥cover：给……保险；annual fee turnover：一年的保险额。
⑦reimbursement of costs in defence of a claim：在诉讼案辩护过程中承担诉讼费用。
⑧QC：Queen's Counsel 的缩写形式，其意为：英国王室法律顾问。

UNIT SEVEN

Text   Who Needs Quality Assurance?

> Quality assurance (QA) is a management system which increases confidence that a material, product or service will conform to specified requirement.①

[1]   The Client for construction might reasonably ask why he should be bothered with quality assurance, which would appear to be more applicable to those who sell consumer goods, such as Jaguar Cars and Marks & Spencer.② After all, the project will have been designed to his requirements: the contractor then has, by contract, to complete the construction in accordance with the drawings and specification, and this is enforceable in law.

[2]   Unfortunately, as many clients know to their cost, procurement of construction is not as simple as that: the existence of a legal contract is no guarantee that the Client will ultimately be satisfied with the completed construction. Nor is it much consolation if the Client eventually obtains compensation by arbitration or through the civil courts.③ Unlike a customer of Marks & Spencer he cannot obtain a satisfactory replacement—he is left with the patched-up original which will probably be a continuing source of irritation and unanticipated expense.④

Unsatisfactory Construction—the Causes

[3]   So what are the causes of unsatisfactory construction? First and foremost—Parties and People.

[4]   By parties we mean the Client and those contracted directly or indirectly to him.⑤ The total number can be considerable, including the lead designer, specialist consultants, the contractor, subcontractors and suppliers of products and materials.

[5]   By people we mean those within the contracted parties who design and construct the Client's project and who have to interact with each other in these processes. And the trouble with people is that they are commonly imprecise when communicating with each other, as much in technical matters as in everyday conversation.⑥

[6]   Multiply the number of people by the number of times they have to communicate in realising a project and the potential number of opportunities for misunderstanding and misinterpretation becomes substantial.

Analysis of the Faults

[7]   So what are the faults and the underlying causes?

[8]   Analysis by the Building Research Establishment of a number of faults has suggested

that most are attributable to design errors and poor workmanship on site-possibly only 10% are due to inadequate products.

[9]   The causes of design faults may include:
- misinterpretation of the Client's needs
- using incorrect or out-of-date information
- misinterpretation of design standards
- poor communication between the various designers
- producing an inadequate, imprecise specification.

[10]   The causes of faults in construction may include:
- misinterpretation of the drawings or specification
- poor communication with suppliers and subcontractors
- poor coordination of subcontracted work
- poor workmanship due to inadequate instructions
- inadequate supervision on site.

Getting It Right First Time

[11]   What can the Client do to get his project right first time? There are three principal actions he can take:
- be actively involved in the project
- be systematic
- require the contracted parties to be systematic.

[12]   The Client must become involved in the project by:
- precisely defining his needs at the outset—vital to the lead designer
- carefully selecting the parties to be contracted
- ensuring that responsibilities are defined.

[13]   To carry out these tasks effectively, the Client must be systematic in his procurement procedure. But, if the Client is being systematic, why not also the contracted parties?⑦ The way to ensure this is to ask them to apply quality assurance.

Applying QA

[14]   The purpose of QA is to increase confidence that a material, product or service will conform to the specified requirements. In the case of construction, these requirements should be spelt out by the Client to the lead designer.

[15]   If a supplier is to apply QA, he must work within a quality system. Briefly, a quality system is a written description of his normal manner of working, in so far as it affects the material, product or service that he supplies. In essence, as well as setting out the standards to which the supplier works, the quality system describes how he achieves those standards. By

following his quality system he has a better chance of getting his output right first time.

The Benefits and Implications of QA

[16]   The main benefit of QA to the client is that he can have greater confidence that his project will be completed:
- on time
- to his requirements
- to budget

and, further, that appropriate attention is paid to all three aspects.

[17]   The principal implications are that the Client must:
- invest more of his time in the project
- accept the need to be systematic himself
- bear any additional first cost.

[18]   The Client should weigh any extra first cost against the reduced risk that the completed project will be:
- delayed—with consequential financial loss
- not to his satisfaction—and may cost extra to correct
- outside his budget.

[19]   Additionally, the Client could refer to the experience of those who have found that QA is cost-effective. They have come to appreciate that a construction contract is only as good as the people and systems backing it.

New Words and Expressions

assurance [əˈʃuərəns]	n.	保证；保险
conform * [kənˈfɔːm]	v.	使符合，使一致；依照
consumer * [kənˈsjuːmə]	n.	消费者，用户
specification * [ˌspesifiˈkeiʃən]	n.	说明书；(pl.) 技术要求，规格
enforceable [inˈfɔːsəbl]	a.	可强制服从的；可实施的
know to one's cost		某人吃亏后才明白
ultimately [ˈʌltimeitli]	ad.	最终地；基本地
procurement * [prəˈkjuəmənt]	n.	实现，获得；达成
consolation [ˌkɔnsəˈleiʃən]	n.	安慰（物）；抚恤（金）
compensation * [ˌkɔmpenˈseiʃən]	n.	赔偿；补偿（金）
arbitration [ˌɑːbiˈtreiʃən]	n.	仲裁；调解
replacement * [riˈ(ː)pleismənt]	n.	替换（物）；补充
irritation [ˌiriˈteiʃən]	n.	不快；激怒

unanticipated	[ʌnæn'tisipeitid]	a.	不可预料的，无法预测的
consultant *	[kən'sʌltənt]	n.	顾问；咨询者
subcontractor	['sʌb'kɔntræktə]	n.	分包商，转包者
imprecise	[impri'sais]	a.	不精确的，不明确的
misinterpretation	[,misintə:pri'teiʃən]	n.	曲解；误释
attributable *	[ə'tribjutəbl]	a.	可归因于…的，由…引起的
inadequate *	[in'ædikwit]	a.	不充足的；不适当的
supervision	[,sju:pə'viʒən]	n.	监督，管理
supplier *	[sə'plai]	n.	供应厂商，供应者
essence	['esns]	n.	本质，实质；精华
in essence			本质上，大体上
set out			制定，打算
budget *	['bʌdʒit]	n.	预算
		v.	编预算
consequential	[,kɔnsi'kwenʃəl]	a.	作为结果的；重大的

Notes

①由 that 引导的从句作名词 confidence 的同位语；conform to 作"符合，遵照"讲。
②Jaguar Cars 生产美洲虎牌轿车的公司名。Marks and Spencer 英国一家著名的连锁商场。
③Civil Court 民事（审判）法庭，法律分为 Civil Law 和 Crime Law，前者指民法，后者指刑法；因此这儿的 Civil Court 是 指专门授理涉及民事纠纷的法庭。
④patch up 作为动词词组作"拼凑"讲，这里的 patched-up 是由此转化而成的分词形容词来修饰名词 original（原物，原始作品）。
⑤contracted ... to him 为分词 短语修饰"those"。contract 此处作及物动词当"订立合约，承包"讲。
⑥as much ... as in everyday conversation 用来对谓语 are commonly imprecise 进行程度的说明，as... as 连接两个不同方面进行程度比较。
⑦why not also the contracted parties? 是一个省略句，完整的句子实际上应该是 why shouldn't the contracted parties be also systematic?

Exercises

Reading Comprehension

I . Choose the best answer.

1. To the client for construction , ignoring the application of QA in construction perhaps leads to _____.

A. unexpected extra spending

B. a completed construction which does not conform to his requirements

C. a lawsuit between the client and the parties responsible for the construction

D. all of the above

2. If the client wants to be actively involved in the project, he must _____.

A. keep close relationship with the designer

B. be certain that there are defined persons or parties to take all the responsibilities in construction

C. express his requirements and needs precisely at the very beginning of the project

D. both B and C

3. A quality system is _____.

A. a management system which can increase the clients' confidence that the completed construction will be in accordance with their requirements

B. a working manual

C. a written description on how a supplier's manner of working affects his service and product

D. one that mainly describes how a supplier achieves the standards to which he must work

4. The main benefit of QA to the client is _____.

A. that he can have greater confidence that his project will be finished

B. to ensure him that his project can be completed on time and be in accordance with his requirements

C. that he needn't pay much attention to the process of construction

D. that he can be involved in the project

5. In the last paragraph, line 1 "refer to" means _____.

A. point to   B. depend on   C. consult   D. ask for

II. Say whether the following statements are True (T) or False (F) according to the text.

(   ) 1. The client for construction trusts more the function of a legal contract than that of QA because he thinks that QA brings no benefits at all for him in construction.

(   ) 2. Among the causes of unsatisfactory construction, the author excludes the possibility that the client himself may cause some trouble in construction.

(   ) 3. The greater the number of people and communicative times, the more possible it is to cause misunderstanding and misinterpretation between people.

(   ) 4. "QA is cost-effective" means that QA is effective only after you've paid for the construction.

(   ) 5. The client should, if necessary, spend any additional cost in order to reduce the risk that the final project will be delayed.

Vocabulary

Ⅰ. Fill in the blanks with the words given below. Change the form if necessary.

> essence, consumer, inadequate, guarantee, define, compensation, attributable,

1. The manufacturers _____ that any faulty parts of the products will be replaced free of charge.
2. _____ specification may cause some design faults.
3. The construction company offered the client $10,000 as _____ for its unsatisfactory product.
4. The rights of a client for construction are well _____ in the contract.
5. In _____, what the client asked for is a completed construction that will conform to his requirements.

Ⅱ. Match the words in Column A with their corresponding definitions in Column B.

A	B
1. budget	a. the settling of a dispute or an argument by the decision of a person or group that has been chosen by both sides
2. procurement	b. to make plans for the careful use of money in a way that will bring most advantages
3. unanticipated	c. unexpected
4. arbitration	d. production
5. output	e. the action of obtaining sth. esp. by efforts

Reading Material A

What Should the Client Do?

The First Steps

Step 1 The Client should designate a member of his staff to be responsible within the organisation for the project. The staff member selected should be suitably versed in the procurement of construction. Furthermore, he should have a thorough understanding of the Client's business activities relevant to the new construction, have the confidence of the Client's senior management, and be given the authority to act for the Client in day-to-day matters relating to the new construction.

Step 2 The Client should appoint a representative to procure the design, construction and commissioning on his behalf.① The Client's representative will usually be a construction professional. In addition, he should have experience of the application of QA to construction and should advise the Client on working systematically in all further matters pertaining to the project.

Step 3 The following should be considered jointly:
- selecting the contract procedure to be adopted
- determining the extent to which QA will be applied to the project. The choice of contract procedure will depend on the type of construction, the time-scale, the Client's financial strategy and so on.

Selecting Consultants

The Client may need to appoint one or more professionals, such as an architect and/or consulting engineer. In addition to the usual requirements of experience appropriate to the envisaged construction and proven capability, the Client should look for commitment to QA.[2] If the quality system has been assessed against specific requirements by an independent certification body and a certificate of conformity has been issued, this is evidence of commitment to QA by the organisation.

Selecting Main Contractors

Although a number of main contractors operate quality systems, it is probable that few will have been given certification by an accredited body.[3] The client's representative should therefore adopt the following procedure:
- require each potential contractor to demonstrate competence, financial soundness and operation of a quality system before being invited to tender (prequalification).[4]
  invite tenders from prequalified contractors.
- shortlist a few contractors on the basis of their bids
- assess in detail the quality systems of the shortlisted contractors
- select the contractor to be engaged

Selecting Suppliers

It will generally be the responsibility of the main contractor to assess the quality systems of their suppliers.

Contractual Aspects

The Client's requirements for QA may be covered by a suitable form of agreement between the contracting parties, rather than by amending standard conditions of contract.

The responsibilities of the contracting parties must be precisely defined. The need or otherwise for quality auditing must be spelt out and potential gaps or overlaps in responsibility avoided.⑤ It is also imperative that the drawings and specification for the work be detailed, clear and consistent within themselves.

Notes on QA requirements
Before defining his requirements the Client should
- be aware of both benefits and implications
- appreciate his involvement and role
- be prepared to accept the discipline required

It will be the task of the Client's representative to prepare the case for QA and to ensure that he has the full support of the Client before QA is adopted for the project. Ultimate benefit is derived where QA is applied overall to a project. Where this is not practicable for whatever reason, a conscious decision should be taken to omit QA for specific aspects.

A potential consultant or main contractor to the Client should operate a quality system, but the Client will wish to be assured that the system is effective and appropriate for the service offered. Such assurance may be given by:
- assessment of the system by the Client or his agent (second party assessment)
- assessment and certification of the system under a recognised and appropriate scheme (third-party assessment). Where available such certification should minimise or obviate further assessment by the Client or his agent.⑥

The Client must also decide to what extent external auditing and documentary evidence are necessary. Because of the cost implications it is wise to restrict both requirements to the essential minimum.

Notes

①业主应该指派一名代表负责设计和建设工作的完成，并且代表业主办理一切事务。
②envisage：面临，面对，展望之意。整句可译为：除了要具备与即将接手的建筑任务相关的一些经验和已经得到证实的一些能力外，客户还应该设法落实质量保证措施。
③accredited：鉴定……为合格的。
④要求每个可能签约的合同商在受邀参与投标前展示他的竞争力，经济实力和质量体系的运行效力。
⑤必须阐明是否需要质量监察并且必须避免责任分派上的空档或重复。
⑥如果有这样一个被认可的系统，那么此项查证工作就应该尽量减少或免去由业主或他的代理人进行更进一步查证工作的麻烦。

Reading Material B

Essential Features of QA

The Fundamental Standard

For most construction work in the UK, the fundamental standard is BS 5750. Quality systems. The relevant three parts cover:

Part 1: design/development, production, installation and servicing
Part 2: production and installation
Part 3: final inspection and test

The significance of BS 5750 is that it has now been successfully applied to a wide range of industries, both manufacturing and service, and it can be assumed that most requirements that could affect quality have now been identified. (Of the three parts of BS 5750, Part 1 has the most requirements and these are shown in the box below.) It remains for these requirements to be related to construction, and this is beginning to happen.

Quality Systems

A quality system is essentially a written description of how the business of a firm (or group of firms) is to be carried out, in so far as it affects the quality of the output. As far as practicable, it should be based on existing practices, amended and supplemented where found necessary to conform with BS 5750.① For example, although it may be existing practice for a builder to examine goods delivered to site, a quality system may require him to record that the goods have been examined. The quality system should take into account relevant standards or other appropriate published documents or standards. A number of trade associations, for example, publish codes and standards. The system should be documented in a quality manual that identifies the actions required by BS 5750 and refers to procedures carried out by the firm.② The manual and procedures should be capable of amendment, as necessary.

Certification and Accreditation

Certification and accreditation give the purchaser additional assurance that what is purchased will conform to the specified quality.

There are two main forms of QA certification:
- quality management—establishes that a quality system conforms to BS 5750
- product conformity—establishes in addition that the product conforms to given standards or technical specifications.

Certification bodies are responsible for carrying out independent (third-party) assessment of firms and for granting and maintaining approval as appropriate. Some bodies operate broad-based schemes; others confine their activities to a distinct industrial sector.[3] The type of certification offered should be carefully examined.

The status of certification bodies is varied. Some are linked to trade associations with little or no user representation. Others have become independent or have been independent from inception, with a majority of user representatives on their governing boards. Where they are sufficiently independent and suitably competent, certification bodies may be accreditated by the National Accreditation Council for Certification Bodies. This Council acts on behalf of the Secretary of State for Trade and Industry and recommends government approval of certification bodies within a specified scope, that is, for stated materials, products or services.[4]

The number of accredited bodies is growing. For the purchaser, accreditation establishes the competence and experience of the certification body and therefore the creditability of suppliers approved by that body.

The requirements of a quality system to BS 5750 : part 1
1. Management responsibility
2. Quality system
3. Contract review
4. Design control
5. Document control
6. Purchasing
7. Purchaser supplied product
8. Product identification and traceability
9. Process control
10. Inspection and testing
11. Inspection, measuring and test equipment
12. Inspection and test status
13. Control of non-conforming product
14. Corrective action
15. Handling, storage, packaging and delivery
16. Quality records
17. Internal quality audits
18. Training
19. Servicing
20. Statistical techniques

Quality Auditing

BS 5750 requires that a quality system be subjected to regular, documented internal audits and to periodic management reviews. This is in addition to routine surveillance by a certification body, as applicable.[5]

The objective is to ensure compliance with the existing documented quality system and to determine whether improvements can be made. In all cases, improvement of the existing system is dependent on taking appropriate corrective action, based on feedback from day-to-day operations.

Notes

① 只要行得通，质量体系应该以现有的实践为基础，并在有必要时进行修正和增补，使之与 BS 5750 相一致。

② 质量体系应该记录于质量手册中，这一手册认同了 BS 57050 所要求的操作行为并且也涉及公司所采取的方法步骤。

③ 有的机构采用的是使用范围较广的鉴定系统，而有的机构的鉴定活动仅限于某个特殊的工业部门。

④ 这个委员会是代表国家工商协会工作的，并且推荐政府批准的鉴定机构，这些鉴定机构限于一定的范围，就是说仅仅对已知的材料、产品和服务进行鉴定。

⑤ 如果可行的话，这还包括由鉴定机构进行的例行监督检查。

UNIT EIGHT

Text 　　　　The Managerial Accountant's
　　　　　　　　Role in Decision Making

[1]　　The managerial accountant's role in the decision-making process is to provide relevant information to the managers who make the decisions. Production managers typically make the decisions about alternative production processes and schedules, marketing managers make pricing decisions, and specialists in finance usually are involved in decisions about major acquisitions of equipment. All of these managers require information pertinent to their decisions. Thus, the managerial accountant needs a good understanding of the decisions faced by those managers.

Steps in the Decision-Making Process

[2]　　1. Clarify the decision problem. Sometimes the decision to be made is clear. For example, if a company receives a special order for its product at a price below the usual price, the decision problem is to accept or reject the order. But the decision problem is seldom so clear and unambiguous. Perhaps demand for a company's most popular product is declining. What exactly is causing this problem? Before a decision can be made, the problem needs to be clarified and defined in more specific terms.

[3]　　2. Specify the criterion. Once a decision problem has been clarified, the manager should specify the criterion upon which a decision will be made. Is the objective to maximize profit, increase market share, minimize cost, or improve public service?[①] Sometimes the objectives are in conflict, as in a decision problem where production cost is to be minimized but product quality must be maintained. In such cases, one objective is specified as the decision criterion—for example, cost minimization. The other objective is established as a constraint—for example, product quality must not fall below 1 defective part in 1,000 manufactured units.

[4]　　3. Identify the alternatives. A decision involves selecting between two or more alternatives. If a machine breaks down, what are the alternative courses of action? The machine can be repaired, or replaced, or a replacement can be leased. Determining the possible alternatives is a critical step in the decision process.

[5]　　4. Develop a decision model. A decision model is a simplified representation of the choice problem. Thus, the decision model brings together the elements listed above: the criterion, the constraints, and the alternatives.

[6]　　5. Collect the data. Selecting data pertinent to decisions is one of the managerial accountant's most important roles in an organization.

[7]　　6. Select an alternative. Once the decision model is formulated and the pertinent data

are collected, the appropriate manager makes a decision.

Quantitative versus Qualitative analysis②

[8]　Decision problems involving accounting data typically are specified in quantitative terms. When a manager makes a final decision, however, the qualitative characteristics of the alternatives can be just as important as the quantitative measures. Qualitative characteristics are the factors in a decision problem that cannot be expressed effectively in numerical terms. To illustrate, suppose Worldwide Airways' top management is considering the elimination of its hub operation in London. A careful quantitative analysis indicates that Worldwide Airways' profit-maximizing alternative is to eliminate the London hub. In making its decision, however, the company's managers will consider such qualitative issues as the effect of the closing on its London employees and on the morale of its remaining employees in the airline's Paris, Atlanta, and Tokyo hubs.

[9]　To clarify what is at stake in such qualitative analyses, quantitative analysis can allow the decision maker to put a "price" on the sum total of the qualitative characteristics. For example, suppose Worldwide Airways' controller gives top management a quantitative analysis showing that elimination of the London hub will increase annual profits by $2,000,000. However, the qualitative considerations favor the option of continuing the London operation.③ How important are these qualitative considerations to the top managers? If they decide to continue the London operation, the qualitative considerations must be worth at least $2,000,000 to them. Weighing the quantitative and qualitative considerations in making decisions is the essence of management.

Obtaining Information: Relevance, Accuracy, and Timeliness

[10]　What criteria should the managerial accountant use in designing the accounting information system that supplies data for decision making? Three characteristics of information determine its usefulness.

[11]　Relevance　Information is relevant if it is pertinent to a decision problem.

[12]　Accuracy　Information that is pertinent to a decision problem must also be accurate, or it will be of little use. This means the information must be precise. Conversely, highly accurate but irrelevant data are of no value to a decision maker.

[13]　Timeliness　Relevant and accurate data are of value only if they are timely, that is, available in time for a decision. Thus, timeliness is the third important criterion for determining the usefulness of information. Some situations involve a trade-off between the accuracy and the timeliness of information. More accurate information may take longer to produce. Therefore, as accuracy improves, timeliness suffers, and vice versa.

[14]　To summarize, the managerial accountant's primary role in the decision-making process is twofold:

1. Decide what information is relevant to each decision problem.

2. Provide accurate and timely data, keeping in mind the proper balance between these often conflicting criteria.

New Words and Expressions

managerial	[ˌmænəˈdʒiəriəl]	a.	管理的；经理的
accountant	[əˈkauntənt]	n.	会计员，会计师
acqusition	[ˌækwiˈziʃən]	n.	取得，获得，获得物
pertinent *	[ˈpəːtinənt]	a.	和…有关的，关于…的，相干的
unambiguous	[ˈʌnæmˈbigjuəs]	a.	不含糊的，明确的
criterion *	[kraiˈtiəriən]	n.	(pl. -ria)（批评，判断的）标准，准则
maximize	[ˈmæksimaiz]	v.	使…增加（扩大）到最大限度；找出…的最高值
minimize *	[ˈminimaiz]	v.	使减到最少，按最小限度估计
constraint *	[kənˈstreint]	n.	约束，强制（力）
defective	[diˈfektiv]	a.	有缺陷（缺点）的，有瑕疵的
representation *	[ˌreprizenˈteiʃən]	n.	表示；描述；代表，代理
formulate *	[ˈfɔːmjuleit]	v.	对…作简洁陈述，有系统地表达；用公式表示
quantitative *	[ˈkwɔntitətiv]	a.	（数）量的，定量的
versus	[ˈvəːsəs]	prep.	与…相对（相比）
qualitative *	[ˈkwɔlitətiv]	a.	性质上的，质量上的；定性的
numerical *	[njuː(ː)ˈmerikəl]	a.	数字的，用数字表示的
elimination	[iˌlimineiʃən]	n.	除去，消灭
hub	[hʌb]	n.	中心，中枢
at stake			利害（生死）悠关，在危险中
option *	[ˈɔpʃən]	n.	选择，取舍；选择权
timely *	[ˈtaimli]	a.	合时的，适时的，及时的
trade-off	[ˈtreidəf]		权衡，交替换位
vice versa			反之亦然
twofold	[ˈtuːfəuld]	a.	两重的，两件事的，两个部分的

Notes

①to maximize profit ... service 动词不定式作表语。
②quantitative analysis 定量分析，数量分析；qualitative analysis 定性分析，质量分析。
③the qualitative considerations 质量因素。consideration 用作复数时作"因素"讲。

Exercises

Reading Comprehension

Ⅰ. Choose the best answer.
1. Throughout the six steps, which of the following is the managerial accountant chiefly responsible for?
   A. clarifying the decision problem
   B. specifying the criterion
   C. collecting the data
   D. selecting an alternative
2. If the objectives in decision making process are in conflict, the decision maker can _____.
   A. select one as a major target and others neglected
   B. make one the criterion and another as a limit that should be observed
   C. choose only one objective after having discussed with the managerial accountant
   D. specify all of the criteria in case
3. What's a hub as for an airline?
   A. one stop on its airways
   B. an overseas office that deals with some business of the company
   C. a large central airport where many of the airline's routes intersect
   D. a station that keeps close contact with the headquarters of the airline
4. In taking the Worldwide Airway as an example, the author is mainly to illustrate _____.
   A. qualitative analysis can be converted into quantitative analysis.
   B. quantitative terms can clarify the decision problem more effectively
   C. how to put six decision-making procedures into practice
   D. the importance of both quantitative and qualitative analysis in making decisions
5. The information obtained by the managerial accountant should be _____.
   A. precise and available in time for a decision first
   B. related to the decision problem first
   C. accurate, relevant and timely in the meantime
   D. none of the above

Ⅱ. Say whether the following statements are True (T) or False (F) according to the text.
  (   ) 1. The main role of the managerial accountant in an organization is to provide information to those decision makers, and the more, the better.
  (   ) 2. The standard upon which the executives make the decision is the objective the organization wishes to achieve in its near future development.

(   ) 3. The decision model is a detailed representation of the decision problem, criterion, the alternatives.

(   ) 4. In terms of accounting data quantitative factors seem rather important and typical than qualitative considerations.

(   ) 5. In the case of Worldwide Airways, it's not an easy job to decide ending the operation of a hub because it involves a series of effects on the other hubs.

Vocabulary

I. Fill in the blanks with the words given below. Change the form if necessary.

> pertinent, criterion, acquisition, maximize, unambiguous,
> minimize, defective, hub, formulate,

1. The major _____ of equipment and staff must be determined by the general manager of the company.
2. _____ information is of no value to the decision makers.
3. The factory lost its competitiveness in the market because it produced too many _____ products.
4. It's very hard to maintain product quality while _____ production cost is desired.
5. A lot of working experience and professional skills are needed when the final-decision maker _____ a decision model.

II. Match the words in Column A with their corresponding definitions in Column B.

A	B
1. option	a. a balance between two opposing situations or qualities intended to produce a desirable result.
2. elimination	b. at risk.
3. pertinent	c. choice, selection
4. trade-off	d. relevant, related
5. at stake	e. get rid of sth. completely or bring sth. to an end

Reading Material A

The Master Budget: a Planning Tool[①]

The master budget, the principal output of a budgeting system, is a comprehensive profit plan that ties together all phases of an organization's operations. The master budget is comprised of many separate budgets, or schedules, that are interdependent.

Sales of Services or Goods

The starting point for any master budget is a sales revenue budget based on forecast sales of services or goods.② Airlines forecast the number of passengers on each of their routes. Banks forecast the number and dollar amount of consumer loans and home mortgages to be provided.③ Hotels forecast the number of rooms that will be occupied during various seasons. Manufacturing and merchandising companies forecast sales of their goods.

Sales Forecasting Sales forecasting is a critical step in the budgeting process, and it is very difficult to do accurately.

Various procedures are used in sales forecasting, and the final forecast usually combines information from many different sources. Many firms have a top-management-level market research staff whose job is to coordinate the company's sales forecasting efforts. Typically, everyone from key executives to the firm's sales personnel will be asked to contribute sales projections.

Major factors considered when forecasting sales include the following:

1. Past sales levels and trends:
   a. For the firm developing the forecast④
   b. For the entire industry
2. General economic trends. (Is the economy growing? How fast? Is a recession or economic slowdown expected?)
3. Economic trends in the company's industry. (In the petroleum industry, for example, is personal travel likely to increase, thereby implying increased demand for gasoline?)
4. Other factors expected to affect sales in the industry. (Is an unusually cold winter expected, which would result in increased demand for home heating oil in northern climates?)
5. Political and legal events. (For example, is any legislation pending in Congress that would affect the demand for petroleum, such as tax incentives to use alternative energy sources?)⑤
6. The intended pricing policy of the company.
7. Planned advertising and product promotion.⑥
8. Expected actions of competitors.
9. New products contemplated by the company or other firms. (For example, has an automobile firm announced the development of a new vehicle that runs on battery power, thereby reducing the demand for gasoline?)
10. Market research studies.

The starting point in the sales forecasting process is generally the sales level of the prior year. Then the market research staff considers the information discussed above along with input from key executives and sales personnel. In many firms, elaborate econometric models are built to incorporate all the available information systematically. (Econometric means economic measurement.). Statistical methods, such as regression analysis and probability distributions for sales, are often used.⑦ All in all, a great deal of effort generally goes into the sales forecast, since it is such a critical step in the budgeting process. Making a sales forecast is like shooting an arrow. If the archer's aim is off by only a fraction of an inch the arrow will go further and further astray and miss the bull's-eye by a wide margin.⑧ Similarly, a slightly inaccurate sales forecast, coming at the very beginning of the budgeting process, will throw off all of the other schedules comprising the master budget.

Notes

①master budget：总预算，主预算。
②a sales revenue budget：销货收入预算。
③home mortgages：住宅抵押贷款。
④the firm developing the forecast：（进行）销售预测的公司。
⑤例如是否国会正在讨论影响石油需求的立法，诸如赋税激励政策以鼓励选用其它能源。
⑥有计划地广告宣传和促销活动。
⑦一些统计学方法如回归分析和销售的概率分布常常被使用。
⑧如果射手的目标偏差毫厘，箭将会越飞越偏，最终会与靶心相差一大截。

Reading Material B

Operational Budgets①

Based on the sales budget, a company develops a set of budgets that specify how its operations will be carried out to meet the demand for its goods or services.

Manufacturing Firms A manufacturing company develops a production budget, which shows the number of product units to be manufactured. Coupled with the production budget are ending-inventory budgets for both work in process and finished goods.② Manufacturers plan to have some inventory on hand at all times to meet peak demand while keeping production at a stable level. From the production budget, a manufacturer develops budgets for the direct materials, direct labor, and overhead that will be required in the production process.③ A budget for selling and administrative expenses is also prepared.

Merchandising Firms The operational portion of the master budget is similar in a merchandising firm, but instead of a production budget for goods, a merchandiser develops a budget for merchandise purchases.④ A merchandiser will not have a budget for direct material, because it does not engage in production. However, the merchandiser will develop budgets for labor (or personnel), overhead, and selling and administrative expenses.

Service Industry Firms Based on the sales budget for its services, a service industry firm develops a set of budgets that show how the demand for those services will be met. An airline, for example, prepares the following operational budgets: a budget of planned air miles to be flown; material budgets for spare aircraft parts, aircraft fuel, and inflight food; labor budgets for flight crews and maintenance personnel; and an overhead budget.

Cash budget Every business prepares a cash budget. This budget shows expected cash receipts, as a result of selling goods or services, and planned cash disbursements, to pay the bills incurred by the firm.

Summary of Operational Budgets Operational budgets differ since they are adapted to the operations of individual companies in various industries. However, operational budgets are also similar in important ways. In each firm they encompass a detailed plan for using the basic factors of production—material, labor, and overhead—to produce a product or provide a service.

Budgeted Financial Statements The final portion of the master budget includes a budgeted income statement, a budgeted balance sheet, and a budgeted statement of cash flows.⑤ These budgeted financial statements show the overall financial results of the organization's planned operations for the budget period.

Nonprofit Organizations The master budget for a nonprofit organization includes many of the components shown above. However, there are some important differences. Many nonprofit organizations provide services free of charge. Hence, there is no sales budget. However, such organizations do begin their budgeting process with a budget that shows the level of services to be provided. For example, the budget for the city of Houston would show the planned levels of various public services.

Nonprofit organizations also prepare budgets showing their anticipated funding. The city of Houston budgets for such revenue sources as city taxes, state and federal revenue sharing, and sale of municipal bonds.

In summary, all organizations begin the budgeting process with plans for (1) the goods or services to be provided and (2) the revenue to be available, whether from sales or from other funding sources.

Notes

①operational budget：业务预算。
②与产量预算联系在一起的还有一份制作过程及制成品的期末库存预算。
③... budgets for the direct materials, direct labor, and overhead... process 可译为：对直接材料成本，直接人工成本和生产过程中所需要的间接管理费的预算。
④merchandise purchases：购货，进货。
⑤a budgeted income statement 收益预算表；a budgeted balance sheet：资产负债预算表。

UNIT NINE

Text   Housing Supply

Definitions

[1]   In any economic analysis which is centred upon market systems of provision, price signals play the critical role in reordering the consumption and production plans of consumers and suppliers of products. Thus, in examining the supply side of the housing system the focus of interest rests upon how the flow of housing price changes. Accepting, for the moment, a flow related definition of housing supply, it is apparent that the rate at which new supplies enter the market can vary with the new house building completion rate or by raising or lowering the rate of flow of housing services from existing stocks of housing.[①] Thus housing supply, even with this simple definition, is likely to be a complex phenomenon with new suppliers or suppliers from existing stock facing different supply technologies or factor prices. That is, new supply and conversion supply may require separate, but interdependent, analysis. Further, since supply reactions will inevitably reflect decision implementation and construction lags, the time period over which supply adjustments are to be analysed must be considered. The market period, following conventional microeconomic terminology, is by definition that period in which flows remain fixed. The short run allows variable factors of supply production to be varied and in the long run, by definition, all inputs and outputs may change. Thus, the general term 'housing supply' is not particularly helpful and analysis has to be directed to specific supply sectors over indicated time periods. Although the most satisfactory conceptual model of housing supply probably relates to a model of the flow of housing services from new and previously existing stock at any point in time, it is difficult to envisage how such a flow or flow adjustment model might be specified and tested. More usually supply analysis is undertaken using a stock adjustment model, where the major concern is with the rate of new additions to housing stocking conversions, improvements and, at the other extreme, housing demolitions and depreciation.

The Economics of the Construction Sector

[2]   British economists have had a long-standing interest in the residential construction sector. However, this interest has generally been expressed with regard to macroeconomic modelling of the behaviour of the national economy. Conversion and rehabilitation, flow adjustment and supply adjustments within urban economies have not been subject to systematic economic analysis. The research agenda for the housing supply sector in North America, as is indicated below, has, on the other hand, generated a considerable volume of empirical and theo-

retical studies of supply in urban housing markets. But in Britain the microeconomic foundations of housing market supply behaviour were seldom, if ever, considered to be of importance per se.

Macroeconomic Significance

[3]   The somewhat simplistic concern with the aggregate demand effects of construction activity is perhaps understandable given the size and cyclical susceptibility of the sector.[2] In 1976, in the United Kingdom, the construction sector produced 15 per cent of gross domestic product and employed an estimated 2.5m. employees. Housing construction is estimated to contribute about one third of overall construction sector output.

[4]   The construction sector is extremely susceptible to the policy actions of central and local governments. Fiscal restraint, reflected in cuts of or restraints on public expenditure, has usually a rapid effect on the public sector building effort, and generally, in Britain, public and private sector starts move together (Table. 9-1). Monetary restraint has generally been reflected in rises in minimum lending rates which have had a pronounced and rapid effect on construction activity because of its almost total dependence upon bank credit to finance construction. These general observations on the size and cyclical characteristics of the construction sector have recently been confirmed for the UK and they are at variance with patterns observed in the USA. In the period prior to 1975 the British construction cycle had a pattern significantly different in detail from the series for aggregate capital formation in the economy as a whole. The British construction cycle responds very quickly to decreases in interest rates in the downturn phase, leading the main series by about one year. The series for construction shows relatively high variability around a rising activity trend with marked peaks and troughs.

Table 9-1   Housing supply in Britain

	Private housing starts (UK)	Local authority housing starts(UK)	Slum clearance E.W. and S.	Values of construction output (Lm. current)		Housing repair and maintenance as % of total housing spending	Extended time lag-start completion(GB) pub. (mths) pvte	
				New housing public	Housing repair private and maintenance			
1965	214,466	188,742	76,200	541	658	484	29	16	0.9
1966	197,241	192,622	83,387	594	652	518	29	16.3	12
1967	237,687	199,923	90,239	670	705	565	30	15.1	12.1
1968	204,768	177,645	90,354	731	782	627	30	15.1	12.3
1969	171,463	156,716	87,080	727	743	639	30	16.3	13
1970	169,154	137,647	85,149	690	737	686	32	16.7	13.7
1971	212,108	122,122	90,611	687	941	765	32	16.8	12
1972	232,190	104,857	84,616	697	1,218	946	33	17.7	11.5
1973	219,847	91,297	80,036	867	1,672	1,279	34	20.2	13
1974	109,604	124,392	55,128	1,122	1,467	1,504	37	20.9	16.4
1975	153,733	139,785	63,044	1,482	1,543	1,658	35	17.9	20.1
1976	158,361	133,663	57,984	1,795	1,798	1,788	33	16.5	17
1977	138,582	96,835	46,518	1,751	1,867	2,106	37	17.7	17.6
1978	161,597	79,519	38,885					19.1	17.7
1979	144,261	57,412	37,036					21.2	17.8

Source: Housing and Construction Statistics.

[5] These fluctuations in housing starts, completion lags and housing completions are indicated in Table 9-1. Quite clearly the late 1970s has been a period of marked recession in residential construction activity, following the record levels of housing output observed earlier in the decade. The sharply cyclical character of the sector reflects the interaction of economic policy with the detailed production processes and input and decision structures within the sector. At the same time such a pattern of fluctuation and 'stop-go' in output also forms the environment in which construction decision takers must operate and the uncertainty generated undoubtedly influences expectations and reactions within the sector. Such influences must be borne in mind as this discussion shifts to a microeconomic perspective first of the industry then firm levels of disaggregation.

New Words and Expressions

vary with	v.	随……而变化
interdependent [intədi'pendənt]	a.	互相依赖的，互相依存的
implementation [implimen'teiʃən]	n.	贯彻，实现
microeconomic ['maikrəu͵jiːkə'nɔmik]	a.	微观经济（上）的
terminology [təːmi'nɔlədʒi]	n.	术语学，术语
short run		短期
sector ['sektɔ]	n.	（尤指商业、贸易等）部门，区域
envisage [in'vizidʒ]	vt.	展望，设想
stock adjustment model		存量调整模型
demolition [͵demə'liʃən]	n.	拆除，破坏
depreciation [diːpriːʃi'eiʃən]	n.	折旧；跌价
long-standing	a.	持久不衰的，长期存在的
rehabilitation ['riːhəbili'teiʃən]	n.	恢复
agenda [ə'dʒendə]	n.	议事日程；记事本
per se [pəː'siː]		本身，本来，本质上
simplistic [sim'plistik]	a.	过分简单化的
understandable ['ʌndəstændəbl]	a.	可懂的，可理解的
aggregate * ['grigit]	a.	合计的，聚集的
	v.	聚集，集合
	n.	集合，聚合
gross domestic product		国民生产总值；国内总产值
cyclical * ['saiklikəl]	a.	周期的，循环的，轮转的
susceptible * [sə'septəbl]	a.	易受影响的，敏感的
fiscal ['fiskəl]	a.	国库的；（美）财政的，公款的
susceptibility [səseptə'biliti]	n.	敏感，感受性
monetary ['mʌnitəri]	a.	钱的，货币的，金融的

pronounced [prəˈnaunst]	a.	显著的，明显的
bank credit		银行信贷
variance * [ˈvɛəriəns]	n.	变化，变动，变异；方差
at variance		（事物间）不符；（人和人）有分歧；不和
variability [vɛəriˈbiliti]	n.	变化性；易变
trough [trɔːf]	n.	商业周期的低潮
fluctuation [flʌktjuˈeiʃən]	n.	起伏，涨落，波动
marked * [mɑːkt]	a.	显著的，清楚的
disaggregation [disəgrəˈgeiʃən]	n.	解集作用，聚集体分开成为它的构成部分
clearance * [ˈkliərəns]	n.	净空，间隙，余隙

Notes

①Accepting, for the moment,... from existing stocks of housing。此句中的"Accepting... housing supply"是现在分词短语作条件状语。主句的主语由"it"充当（形式主语），而真正的主语是由"that the rate... stocks of housing"引起的 主语从句。然而主语从句中的主语"the rate"又带有一个限制性定语从句。"can vary"为其谓语，"or"连接的是两个等立成份，"with the new..."和"by... stocks of housing"分别作状语。

②The somewhat simplistic concern.... cyclical susceptibility of the sector。此句中的"given the size and... of the sector"是过去分词短语作状语；"given"意为"考虑到"。

Exercises

Reading Comprehension

Ⅰ. Choose the best answer.

1. From the second paragraph, we can learn that _____.
    A. the British people are interested in the residential construction sector
    B. the North Americans have succeeded in the housing supply sector
    C. the British economists have learned something from the research agenda for the housing supply sector in North America
    D. so far as the economics of the construction sector is concerned, the British and the North American take different point of views

2. In the last sentence of paragraph two, the word per se means _____.
    A. considered alone and not in connection with other things
    B. something that has a particular quality simply because it is what it is
    C. taking into account the practical aspects or your own experiences

D. none of the above

3. In 1976, housing construction consists of _____ of gross domestic product.
   A. 2.5million   B. 85%   C. 15%   D. 5%

4. Read Table 9-1, compare 1965 with all the years in the table you can conclude that _____ in Britain because of the effect of the policy actions of finance.
   A. the public starts move faster than the private
   B. the private starts move in the opposite direction to the public
   C. the public and private starts move in the same rhythm, up or down
   D. the public starts have nothing to do with the private

5. Again from Table 9-1, we can learn that the late 1970s has been at a low ebb in construction sector in the UK, which implies that _____.
   A. British people have no longer been interested in construction for they have no housing problems
   B. British people have better way to make money than developing construction sector
   C. Britain has been in economic recession
   D. the construction sector is limited to man power

II. Say whether the following statements are True (T) or False (F) according to the text.

(　) 1. In terms of any economic analysis, price signals, in the market, crucially influence rearrangement of production and consumption.

(　) 2. From the first paragraph, we can learn that based on individual supply sectors and different time periods, supply analysis must be specified.

(　) 3. The UK is more microeconomic, but the North America is more macroeconomic.

(　) 4. The construction sector is insusceptible to the policy actions of central and local governments.

(　) 5. In general, construction activity is financially aided by national financial support.

Vocabulary

I. Match the words in Column A with their corresponding definitions in Column B.

A	B
1. aggregate	a. probability that something will vary
2. cyclical	b. related to public money, taxes, debts, etc.
3. variability	c. the distance between one object and another passing beneath or beside it
4. clearance	d. collected into one group, total, or mass
5. fiscal	e. happening in cycles

II. Complete the following sentences with some of the words listed below. Change the form if necessary.

> implementation, depreciation, envisage,
> rehabilitation, fluctuation

1. The last forecast _____ inflation falling to about 10 percent.
2. He did not do enough to secure the _____ of residential construction.
3. Runaway inflation has caused the _____ of the country's currency.
4. The government tried best to avoid the _____ of the money market.
5. There was no money to accomplish the _____ of old streets in the city.

Reading Material A

Industrial Structure/Low Productivity Growth

Industrial Structure

The industry has an industrial structure which could be described as being deconcentrated and there are a large number of very small firms. There are some statistical pitfalls in comparing the size structure of the industry at different points in time, but Table 9-2 indicates that this size structure has remained quite stable over the time period 1964-1976.① However, this scenario of structural stability and low concentration is perhaps less obvious at the level of individual or regional housing markets. For instance, although a regional housing market may contain a variety of firm types such as small local firms, medium sized local firms, branches of national companies and headquarters of building giants, the number and range of firms able to respond to local opportunities at a specific time period, taking into account the ongoing commitments of existing firms, may be limited.② Thus, an apparently competitive industrial structure may, at the local level, display imperfections in responses. There is also growing evidence that, at least in some British regions, the larger firms are now producing an ever-increasing share of residential construction output even if the number of such firms is now declining.

The statistics presented for the size structure of the industry do not necessarily imply that local housing market supply will be provided by atomistically competitive supply.③ Neoclassical analysis of housing supply has, as one might expect, considered the ownership structure or concentration characteristics of the industry as being a likely guide to supply behaviour. A deconcentrated pattern of ownership was interpreted as ensuring the safe use of a model of a competitive market immediately adjusting to housing market conditions with perfect information. This equation of market structure and economic behaviour, which is examined in detail below, has historically been used to predict the locations, density and timing of new housing supply.

Table 9-2   Private construction firms, by size Great Britain, 1965~1978

	1965	1970	1973 A	1973 B	1975	1978
0-1	18 488	20 355	17 785	29 563	28 131	28 551
2-7	38 774	33 118	32 574	43 962	39 079	42 007
8-13	10 581	7 946	8 342	9 311	8 516	9 092
14-24	7 164	5 358	5 853	6 315	5 667	5 712
25-34	2 648	1 982	2 224	2 364	2 058	1 945
35-59	2 798	2 062	2 203	2 298	2 050	1 918
60-79	894	720	707	743	674	620
80-114	790	616	675	697	609	549
115-229	1 040	820	856	872	801	733
300-599	290	233	239	246	234	224
600-1 199	149	132	125	125	127	115
1 200+	80	78	80	80	71	54
All firms	83 696	73 420	71 663	96 576	88 017	91 520

Low Productivity Growth

The construction sector has low levels and growth rates of labour productivity. It is generally considered that the continued survival of a large number of small construction firms reflects the fact that construction is essentially an on-site activity which must use traditional and specialised labour inputs and materials and which allow few scale economies to emerge in the production process.[4] In some respects the site supervising firm, or general contractor, comes very close to the Coasian notion of a firm. That is, Coase perceives the firm to be a decision locus responsible for organizing and co-ordinating a large number of contracts for specialised inputs over fixed but varying, production periods. Industrialised building, at least in the United Kingdom, had largely been restricted to the public sector. Even within the public sector, industrialised building seldom exceeded more than a fifth of starts of completions in a given period and between 1974 fell from 18.8 per cent of public starts to 4.6 per cent in 1979 (in a considerably reduced volume of public sector starts). Though it is true, however, that in the private sector there is an increasing tendency to substitute inputs which have been produced in off-site situations of potential scale economies, for on-site production. For instance, plasterboard replaces on-site plastering, prehung doors and aluminium window frames reduce on-site joinery inputs, etc.

Supply in the Housing System

However, the capacity of the construction sector to further develop offsite preparation is largely related to the ability to produce and sell standardised output. Craven (1970) suggests that such adjustment is largely restricted to firms which are already large scale and which build semidetached and terraced houses on large-scale sites (usually on the suburban fringes of cities). Smaller, more local companies are restricted to producing diversified output on smaller sites.

Notes

① 虽然在不同的时期，对工业规模结构进行比较时，往往有些统计方面的错误，但是，表 9-2 却表明在 1964～1976 这段时期，这种规模结构一直相当稳定。

② 例如，尽管地区房产市场会包含各种类别的公司．如小型地方公司，中型地方公司，国家公司的分公司以及建筑公司的总部；然而，若将现有公司正承担的义务考虑在内，在某个具体时期，能对本地建筑场所提供的机遇作出反应的公司的数量和范围（规模）可能是有限的。

本句是一个含有让步状语从句的主从复合句。状语从句是 "although a regional... at a specific time period"，主句是 "the number and range... may be limited"。其中 "taking into account... of existing firms" 是分词短语作条件状语。而 "... able to respond... at a specific time period" 是 "firms" 的定语。

③ 工业规模结构的统计资料表明，地方房产市场的供给并不一定是靠分散性的竞争供给所提供。

④ 人们一般认为，大量的小型建筑公司能持续生存下来反映出一个事实，即建筑基本上说是一种现场活动，它必须使用传统和特别的劳动投入以及建筑材料。在生产过程中，它几乎不允许有规模的经济活动出现。本句中 "that clause" 是 "the fact" 的同位语。另外，同位语从句中的两个由 which 引出的从句都是 "activity" 的定语。

Reading Material B

Speculative Building/The Construction Firm

Speculative Building

The finance of construction is only one of several factors contributing to the instability of the industry. Most residential construction is speculative. That is, producers generally do not build to order, but instead adjust housing starts and completions in relation to demand conditions and price and cost expectations. ① When demand is on the downswing firms may lengthen completions lags, by reducing overtime, etc, and may quickly reduce starts. For instance in the 1970s, average completions lags for the private housing sector varied from |5--2| months (Table 9-3). Financing arrangements demand this rapid adjustments and the low fixity of labour inputs enable it. By such rapid adjustments construction firms may lessen or indeed forestall completely price reductions on their speculative output nearing the completion phase. In periods of demand expansion, speculative builders may require to have firm price expectations before raising completion rates and initiating new starts. Since general monetary expansion has a very rapid effect on housing demand, it is not surprising that house price rises accompany monetary expansion as the supply response decision is subject to numerous lags. ②

These are all important characteristics of the housing construction sector. But they are in no way a recent set of phenomena. In an analysis more than two decades ago, Carter (1958) attributed the preponderance of small firms to the 'smallness of jobs', the ease of entry into the sector for craftsmen and the ease of buying specialised services. At the same time he observed that construction was a complex-phased production process in which there were no apparent economies of scale, whereas self-site supervision led to obvious managerial economies. At that time Carter described the construction industry as 'an untidy and shambling giant, with some difficulty in co-ordinating the movement of its limbs so that it may move forward'. ③ This description still seems apposite. Therefore, although the industrial economics characteristics of the construction sector yield some insights, it is important to consider in more detail the production decision which actually faces a representative construction firm.

The Construction Firm

It has already been suggested that economic analysis of the construction sector in the UK is extremely limited and this lack of knowledge reflects an inadequate understanding of the basic decision making units within the sector. ④ ' Surprisingly little is known about the way decisions are made in individual firms, or the effect these may have on opportunities for owner occupation'.

In this section it is intended to draw attention to the complexity of the construction process. It is hoped that this detailed view of a construction firm will point out the extreme reductionist thinking which lies behind the simple neoclassical presentation of the building industry as being composed of a series of perfectly competitive firms through which economic 'causes' (house price changes) smoothly trigger supply responses. ⑤

Just as the previous chapters have stressed the need for the analysis or adjustment processes in the housing choice decision of household, so this section draws attention to the inherent imperfections and uncertainties of the construction processes which condition the pattern, over time and space, of housing development.

Notes

① 这就是说，开发商通常并不刻意安排指令工程的破土和完工，而是根据需求状况、价格以及预期成本来调节工程的破土和完工的。

② 既然货币的增长对房屋需求有着非常迅速的影响，那么当供给关系受到多种滞后因素的制约时，房价仍然伴着货币的增长而增长，这就不足为奇了。

③ 那时，卡特将建筑工业说成是一个"不修边幅且步履蹒跚的巨人。由于在协调四肢的活动方面有些困难，所以进展缓慢"。

④ 早已有人认为，在英国，对建筑部门的经济分析是十分有限的。对这方面的无知反映出人们对部门内部的决策机构不甚了解。

⑤ 希望这种对建筑公司的详细说明能指出那些极端简化主义者的一种偏见，这种偏见的产生是因为受到新古典主义对建筑工业的简单描述的影响。认为建筑工业是由一系列竞争性的公司所组成，通过这些公司的各种经济活动（如房价的变化）就能顺利地引起供给方面的各种反响。lies behind：是……的原因。

UNIT TEN

Text   Construction

[1]   The actual construction phase may take from twelve months to four years to complete and the completions rate may be used as a variable by the firm to adjust to changing demand conditions. As noted above, in periods of brisk demand the completions rate may be accelerated by overtime working, etc. to ensure quick sales, and in periods of recession in the housing market reduced labour inputs per unit of time will allow a slower completion rate so that builders may avoid the policing and financial costs of holding stocks of vacant completed houses.①

[2]   Undoubtedly the construction firm requires substantial managerial skills to reach efficiently the stage of project development when construction can actually commence. But the actual organization of construction requires considerable effort to phase and implement a whole series of small-scale contracts. Table 10-1 indicates the great variety of trades and skills, often provided by small subcontractors, required to produce a house (see Fig. 10-1).② This large number of small-scale inputs suggests that inefficiencies and indivisibilities in labour use are likely to be a characteristic problem in the industry. This complexity is exacerbated by specific phasing required for on-site construction with, for example, structural workers being required predominantly in the middle phases of development.③ Clearly a large-scale site operator with a large number of houses at various stages of completion can use specific labour inputs more systematically than smaller firms. Smaller firms, and indeed many larger firms, overcome this problem of technical variations in demand for specific skills by extensive short-term subcontracting. However, efficiency of labour use, in these cases, may only be obtained by exacerbating the difficulties and delays of setting up the construction activity via a myriad of small contracts. Small, nonunionised firms, may overcome many of these phasing difficulties if employees perform a variety of tasks. For instance labouring, joinery, roofing and finishing which may require specific trade inputs in unionised firms may be undertaken by the same individuals in smaller firms.

The Labour Market

[3]   Reference has already been made to the mix of skills and subtle phasing of labour inputs required in the construction. It was further suggested that the complex pattern of labour inputs posed problems for improving efficiency in the sector. It is this issue of efficiency, and more particularly efficiency wages which are highlighted here. Clearly sustained wage inflation poses particular problems for planning and management in an industry with low productivity growth and a relatively irreducible share of labour inputs in the physical production process.

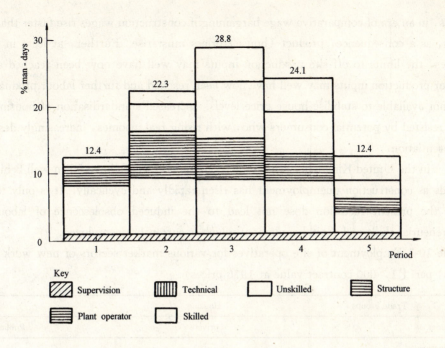

Fig. 10-1 Complexity of phasing labour inputs for construction.
Source: NEDO. (1977: 6, 63.)

[4] Low productivity growth in housing construction has always been a concern in the UK and has also been a source of comment in other economies (Stegman 1970). This low productivity growth has been variously attributed to poor management, to the failure of technological progress to be introduced at the design stage and to conservative labour practises in the labour force which has particularly high turnover rates.④ All these arguments seem plausible but detailed empirical verification is, once again, lacking.

[5] The inflationary experience of the 1970s has made the productivity issue of particular significance. Construction sector wage statistics indicate that wage rates in the sector expanded at approximately the national average rate until 1977, though recent experience has seen construction wages fall well below national levels. In general, construction hours worked per week exceed average hours per week and the index of industrial production suggests that output per man in the construction sector lags behind the national average. This low rate of output per man cannot, of course, be assumed to arise because of low-skilled manpower. Land conditions, capital used and management skills all affect average output per man (or machine or acre). Strenuous efforts have been made to seek out productivity improvements in building, and in particular off-site mass production of components (see above) is viewed as a potential, but limited, source of productivity gain. Howerer, Stegman, citing the Baumol model of sectoral unbalanced growth, was not optimistic about the potential for improving productivity in America in the 1970s.

[6] The construction industry is an industry where labour inputs are clearly fundamental.

Thus, in an era of comparative wage bargaining if construction wages rise faster than efficiency then, as a consequence, product (house) prices must rise. Further, at least in the United States, the limits to off-site production inputs may well have now been reached and further labour production inputs may well have now been reached and further labour productivity gains are not available to stabilise house price levels. Increased standardisation of housing output is also resisted by potential consumers who, with rising real incomes, increasingly desire product differentiation.

[7] In the United Kingdom, at present, construction wages have fallen well behind national trends as construction unemployment has risen rapidly and cyclically. It is only to be hoped that the present recession dose not lead to the induced obsolescence of labour and entrepreneurial skills and capital equipment which is currently unemployed.

Table 10-1 Employment of site operatives for various market sectors of new work (site mandays* per £1,000 contract value at 1970 prices)

Trade groups	Housing	
Trades	private	Public
Structure		
Bricklayer	9.1	9.0
Roofer	1.1	0.9
Steel erector	—	0.3
Erector	—	0.3
Glazier	0.2	0.2
Others	0.2	
Total	10.6	10.4
Carpenter	8.3	7.9
Services		
Plumber	2.8	2.5
Heating	0.2	0.8
Electrician	1.8	2.5
Others	0.2	0.4
Total	5.0	6.2
Finishes		
Plasterer	4.2	3.7
Painter	4.5	4.6
Floorlayer	0.5	0.5
Others	0.8	0.4
Total	10.0	9.2
Other		
General labourer	14.5	16.8

Plant operator	2.0	1.1
Scaffolder	0.8	0.3
Steelfixer	—	0.3
Welder		
Pipelayer	0.2	0.8
Drainlayer		
Tarmac/Asphalt	0.2	0.2
Others	0.8	0.4
Total	18.5	19.9
Gen. Foreman	3.3	3.0
All trades	55.7	56.6

8.5 hours per day (5.5 days per week) for building
Sourcer NEDO 977：29

New Words and Expressions

police [pəˈliːs]	v.	管治；控制；监视
managerial [ˌmænəˈdʒiəriəl]	a.	管理上的，经营上的
commence * [kəˈmens]	v.	开始
implement * [ˈimplimənt]	vt.	实现 实施
inefficiency [ˌiniˈfiʃənsi]	n.	无效；无能
indivisibility [ˈindiˌviziˈbiliti]	n.	不可分性
exacerbate [eksˈæsəːbeit]	vt.	使（病，痛等）加重
short-term	a.	短期的
subcontract [ˈsʌbˈkɔntrəkt]	v.	转包工作，分包合同
myriad [ˈmiriəd]	n.	无数，极大数量
unionize [ˈjuːnjənaiz]	vt.	使成立联合组织；使成立工会
joinery [ˈdʒɔinəri]	n.	细木工技术（或行业）；细木工
roof [ruːf]	v.	给…盖上屋顶，做…的屋面
pose * [pəuz]	v.	提出，形成
highlight	v.	集中注意力于，着重
sustained [səsˈteind]	a.	持久的，持续的，持久不变的
irreducible [ˌiriˈdjuːsəbl]	a.	不能降低（或削减）的，不能缩小的
turnover	n.	（工人）人员更新；产出
plausible [ˈplɔːzəbl]	a.	似乎有理的，似乎可能的
verification * [verifiˈkeiʃən]	n.	证据，证实
inflationary [inˈfleiʃənəri]	a.	膨胀的；通货膨胀的
strenuous [ˈstrenjuəs]	a.	奋发的，使劲的

make strenuous efforts		尽全力
cite * [sait]	v.	引用，引证；传讯
sectoral ['sektərəl]	a.	部分的，部门的；扇形的
stabilize, -ise * ['steibilaiz]	v.	稳定，安定
differentiation [ˌdifərənʃi'eiʃən]	n.	分化，变异；区别
induce * [in'djuːs]	vt.	引起，导致；引诱，劝使
obsolescence [ˌɔbsə'lesns]	n.	废弃，废退；逐渐过时
entrepreneurial [ˌɔntrə'prəːnərəl]	a.	企业家的，关于企业家的

Notes

①句中的 As noted above 是省略了部分句子成份的非限制性定语从句，修饰整个主句，若写完整则应该是"As is noted above"。主句是由"and"连接的两个并列分句构成，其中"the completions rate"是第一个分句的主语；"reduced labor inputs per unit of time"是第二个分句的主语.第二个分句中还含有一个由"so that"引导的目的状语从句。

②本句是个简单句。"often provided by..."和"required to..."都是分词短语作"trades and skills"的定语。

③本句中的"required for... in the middle phases of development"是分词短语作"phasing"的定语，其中"with structural workers being required... in the middle phases of development"又是介词短语作"on-site construction"的定语。

④句中的短语"attribute to"意为"把……归因于；把……归咎于"，它的后面带有三个并列宾语，即：1. poor management 2. the failure... at design stage 3. conservative labor practises... turnover rates。

Exercises

Reading Comprehension

I . Choose the best answer.

1. The main idea of the first paragraph is that _____.

    A. demand conditions meet housing supply

    B. the completions rate of construction is decided by demand conditions

    C. housing supply decides on demand conditions

    D. the estimated construction phase varies from one year to four years

2. When it comes to actual operation of construction, one of the leading factors is _____.

    A. man power

    B. construction rate

    C. advanced machinery

D. skills of management

3. In the sentence "Table 10-1 indicates the great variety of trades and skills,....", "trade" here refers to _____.
   A. services between people, firms or countries
   B. the activity of buying, selling, or exchanging goods
   C. the people or businesses involved in a particular kind of work
   D. transaction

4. In the sentence "Reference has already been made to ... subtle...", the word "subtle" means _____.
   A. difficult to describe because it is delicate
   B. sensitive
   C. pleasantly delicate and faint
   D. complex

5. What will happen if wages in construction sector rise faster than its efficiency?
   A. House prices have to rise
   B. More people will stream into construction sector
   C. Construction sector will have more labor inputs than it needs
   D. Construction sector will ruin the balance of the national economy

II. Say whether the following statements are True (T) or False (F) according to the text.
   (　) 1. In the housing market, more or less labor inputs show that construction industry is in periods of prosperity or recession.
   (　) 2. The ideal solution to inefficiencies and indivisibilities is, first of all, to try to improve the qualities of labor force.
   (　) 3. Efficiency of labor use can be raised by short-term subcontracting.
   (　) 4. The low productivity growth is due to the failure to introduce technological progress.
   (　) 5. In the UK, compared with others, construction industry goes inefficiently with longer work hours and lower wages.

Vocabulary

I. Match the words in column A with their corresponding definitions in column B.

A	B
1. stabilize	a. lead or cause sb to do sth.
2. verification	b. put forward for discussion
3. pose	c. prove or evidence
4. implement	d. become firm, steady or unchanging
5. induce	e. put into practice

II. Complete the following sentences with the words given below. Change the form if necessary.

> commence, phase, inflationary, accelerate, potential

1. The _____ uses of the new material range from floor titles to manhole covers.
2. It's reported that inflation rates began to _____.
3. The construction cycle responds very quickly to decreases in interest rates in the downturn _____.
4. When land and capital market trends are taken into account and planning permission granted, contracts are prepared and finalised and on-site construction is then able to _____.
5. Productivity performance and capacity adjustment behavior of material supply industries will have an important bearing on _____ propensities.

Reading Material A

Materials

The influences of the capital, land and labour markets on the housing construction industry have been recognised by economists working in the areas of monetary, labour and land economics. However, the significance of materials has been less well recognised and this is an important omission. Material inputs commonly constitute at least 40 per cent of the value of construction output and thus form an important linkage between the industrial economy and the housing sector. Clearly productivity performance and capacity adjustment behaviour of material supply industries will have an important bearing on inflationary propensities and builders' reaction rates in housing construction.①

These problems became more apparent when the nature of materials inputs for the construction sector is considered. Aggregates for roads, flooring and foundations are extracted from sites or quarries which are only expanded or initiated after considerable scrutiny from the planning system.② In periods of expansion delays often exceeding eighteen months may be encountered in the planning process. With respect to cement, there are problems in periods of both expanding and contracting demand. When demand for cements is falling, producers have a limited stockpiling capacity as cement cannot be stored for periods exceeding three months. Thus, when a subsequent expansion commences, not only are there limited stocks available, but further, producers have to be convinced that the expansion in demand will be sustained before expanding productive capacity. Even if producers expectations are elastic, the development of major new capacity may take four to five years with 50 per cent of this delay being due to the problems of acquiring planning permission. In the UK cement deliveries had fallen by 14 per cent per year between 1973 and 1977, then rose by 3 per cent in 1978 and 1979 but have since reportedly dropped considerably. The supply of bricks is compounded by similar difficulties and is particularly sensitive to fluctuations in housing demand as production is primarily for housing construction and because, in periods of recession, the cost structure of operating plants is such that capacity usage of less than 80 per cent is usually uneconomical.③

Similar problems arise in relation to the provision of other inputs such as steel, glass and soft wood but they are less severe because of importing possibilities and because housing demand is a lower proportion of the final demand for such products. In conclusion it should be stressed that unstable demand for house-building materials may generate increasing unit costs of production in periods of recession and rising prices and lags in increasing output in periods of expansion.④ Further, local or regional shortages and surpluses of building materials, at least for aggregates, stone, cement and bricks, will cause particular difficulties as these commodities have a low value to bulk (weight) ratio and are therefore costly to transport across regions.

The above discussion has suggested that the construction industry is particularly susceptible to short-run variations in macroeconomic policy and that the industry faces, because of low productivity growth, difficult operating conditions when wage inflation is pervasive. Further, a series of major links into the markets for land and materials were identified. The materials market was seen to be subject to substantial lags in increasing output and the land market was viewed as being subject to phases of destabilising speculation in inflationary economies. Thus, apart from the inherent difficulties of assessing demand, the construction firm is faced with a constantly changing environment of factor prices and availabilities. Hopefully this description has been illuminating per se but it has a further purpose, namely, to provide a back cloth against which the theoretical and applied economic models of construction can be evaluated.

Notes

① 显然，生产效率的高低和材料供应工业的调节能力的强弱，对于通货膨胀及建筑者们在房屋建筑中的反应速度关系极大。
② 用于筑路，室内地面及打地基的混凝土中的配料是在采石场开采的，而采石场的发展或开发只有在对规划系统进行了相当仔细的研究之后才可决定。
③ 与上述困难一样，砖的供给问题更糟糕，因为房屋需求量的波动，对砖的供给有很大的影响。生产砖主要为了建房，同时在衰退时期，生产厂家的成本结构决定了在设备利用率低于80％时，通常是不经济的。
④ 句中的"generate"一词意为"生产"，是及物动词。它在句中有三个宾语。即：1. increasing unit costs... of recession 2. rising prices 3. lags in ... periods of expansion. 最后，应强调的是，建筑材料需求的不稳定会使衰退时期生产的单位成本增加，价格上涨，并且使发展时期的产量增加出现多种延缓情况。

Reading Material B

The Land Market and the Planning System

In urban economic analysis the land market is ascribed the crucial role in shaping the supply of housing. In Marxian analyses of the housing system the land market is ascribed an important and complex role in social and economic processes over space and time. Here it is stressed that the land market is only one of several complex subsystems in the environment of the building firm and thus comment on the market is restricted.

Land and land preparation costs form an increasingly important component of new housing costs and prices. Small sample statistics published by the Nationwide Building Society, by region, show the percentage of plot price in selling price as indicated in Table 10-4. More definitive figures for Scotland indicate that this proportion rose from 9.5 per cent in 1971 to 15.7 percent in 1976. For the UK the DOE land price index (1970=100) rose to 300 in 1973, had fallen back to 200 in 1975 and did not begin to rise again until 1977, but had reached an index of 366 by the end of 1979 following a mini-boom in 1978 and 1979.

Attempts to disentangle the relationships between the earlier land price and house price booms of the 1970s have been somewhat unconvincing. Was there a sudden realisation of landowner monopoly power? Did rises in house prices follow as a consequence from rising land costs or did land prices soar as the result of anticipation of housing development? In the UK these are still open and important research issues. Whatever the order of events, monetary expansion in the UK resulted in speculative rises in land prices, reflecting in part the relatively restricted supply of development land.

Clearly the price elasticity of land supply is generally low but it varies by submarket and housing sector. The construction industry claims, however, that land stocks held by builders are currently some 25 per cent below desired levels, and that land-banking is essential for the orderly progress of the industry.[1] As a response they further add, that the Community Land Act, Development Land Tax and local government reorganisation have so disrupted the supply of land for building that current sales are of a low order and are in general locationally marginal unserviced land.

From the academic viewpoint these somewhat polemical 'assertions' have no status other than as hypotheses.[2] At the present time discussion of the relationship between housing and land markets in the UK is somewhat long on 'hypotheses' and considerably short of 'research'. Specialists in this area of urban economic analysis particularly land economists, may feel that the brief treatment of land attributes derisory significance to the land market. No such implication is intended, the present volume requires a comprehensive consideration of construction and the land market is only one of several significant intended, the residential development process. It is enough for our purposes to note that land planning controls generate lags in developers' responses, that planning standards may raise development costs, and that fluctuations in and a rise of land prices have resulted in land prices becoming an increasingly important and fluctuating element in builders' costs. [3]

When land and capital market trends are taken into account and planning permission granted, contracts are prepared and finalised and on-site construction is then, finally, able to commence. [4] This delay in building starts may, as indicated in Table 10-3, take from eighteen months, at the very least, to five years. Over this time period, demand estimates may be revised and the availability and cost of inputs markedly altered. The construction firm, at the very most, can only hope that it has made a 'best first move' when it starts a construction project.

Table 10-3　　　　　　　　　　　　**lags in the construction sector**

(a) Characteristic times involved in the various phases of the construction process (years)

	Conceptual Design Phase	contract documentation phase	Construction on site phase
Public sector housing	1-4	1-3	1-4
private sector housing	1\2-6	1\2-4	1\2-1.5

(b) Maximum rate of increase possible in material supply

Stocks	Alterations in rate of working existing capacity — Production units with spare capacity	Additions to capacity — Mothballed plants	small plants	large pants	'planning problems'
Less than 1 month	temporarily up to 10%	—	—	—	—
3 months	Up to 10%	—	—	—	—
3-12 months	Up to about 30%	up to +about 30% +	—	—	—
1-2 years			3% or more	—	—
2-3 years				3% or more	—
5 years					3% or more

Provided that there is adequate spare capacity and skilled staff have been retained.
+Provided that there is adequate spare capacity
Source: NEDO (1977, 6, 63)

Table 10-4 **Average prices of new property on which the society approved loans in the first quarter of 1977**

Region	New properties			
	Average prices (£)	Change in indices over past year (%)	Average values of sites (£)	Site values as proportion of price (%)
London & S. East	16,213	(+10)	3,635	22.4
Southern	15,533	(+9)	3,565	23.0
South Western	12,490	(+9)	2,163	17.3
Midland	13,026	(+13)	2,884	22.1
Eastern	12,841	(+11)	2,611	20.3
North Western	12,679	(+13)	2,373	18.7
North Eastern	11,272	(+11)	1,968	17.5
Scotland	14,625	(+11)	2,144	14.7
Wales	12,692	(+9)	1,981	15.6
Northern Ireland	15,856	(+21)	1,923	12.1
United Kingdom	13,586	(+11)	2,692	19.8

Source：Nationwide Building Society Occasional Bulletin 141. April 1977

Notes

①然而，建筑界却声称建房者所拥有的建房土地大约低于当前期望值的25%；地产银行对该工业有条不紊地发展起着举足轻重的作用。

②从学术观点来看，这些带有争议性的"断言"除了可视为假设外，是没有什么其它价值的。

③句中的"note"一词意为"注意"是及物动词。它后面带有三个宾语从句。即：1) that land ... developers' responses 2) that planning standards ... development costs 3) that fluctuations ... builder's costs 这足以让我们注意到土地规划的控制会延缓开发商的反应，各种规划标准会增加开发成本；地价的波动和上涨已使得地价成为建房商成本中一个日趋重要的不稳定因素。

④在考虑了土地和资本市场动向，规划被认可，合同准备就绪并签署之后，才能开始现场施工。

UNIT ELEVEN

Text   Accounting

Accounting: a Dynamic Discipline

[1]   Accounting involves the collection, summarization and reporting of financial data. It is a dynamic discipline, in which new principles and procedures are constantly evolving. The objective of this text is to provide its readers—presumably current and future managers and investors—with the knowledge and skills necessary to take full advantage of accounting information. They should be able to use it in planning, controlling and evaluating the activities of the organizations as well as in making personal and corporate investment decisions. They should be aware not only of the wealth of information that financial reports can provide, but equally important, be cognizant of their limitations[1]. They should, at the very least, be able to know when to consult accounting specialists and to ask the right questions of them.

Objectives of Accounting

[2]   Accounting is concerned with the description of economic events, with the measurement of economic values, and with the determination of periodic changes in such values. It aims to provide information that serves several broad purposes. Among them are:

[3]   1. Allocating the scarce resources of our society. Under any form of economic arrangement, be it capitalism or socialism, decisions as to where capital should be invested are made on the basis of information contained in financial statements.[2] In a free enterprise system, private investors make determinations as to the stock of companies they purchase largely on the basis of data contained in periodic reports of earnings. Bankers and other suppliers of funds study financial reports before making loan decisions. Government agencies decide whom to tax and whom to subsidize on the basis of financial reports.

[4]   2. Managing and directing the resources within an organization. Managers of profit and nonprofit entities alike rely upon accounting information to assure that they maintain effective control over both their human and material resources and to make certain that within their organizations they allocate such resources to the products, subunits, or functions where they can be most productive.

[5]   3. Reporting on the custodianship of resources under the command of individuals or organizations. Individuals, acting either as investors or merely as citizens, entrust resources to professional managers and governmental officials. They expect such managers or officials to provide them with periodic reports be which their performance in office can be evaluated.

Focus on Future

[6]　Accounting focuses on the measurement and communication of a wide range of financial data. Accountants provide the information required to make decisions as to where to allocate financial resources.③ And once such decisions are made they provide the dada necessary to effectively control such resources. Periodically, as the management process is being carried out, accountants "report the score" -they provide information by which the results of prior decisions can be evaluated.

[7]　Viewed from a slightly different perspective, accounting aims to enable managers, investors, creditors, and other users of financial statements to determine the future earning power of an enterprise. Decisions made today can affect only the future, not the past. Those who seek information from financial statements are primarily concerned with how well the enterprise will perform in the years to come rather than those gone by.

[8]　What will occur in the future, however, can best be predicted by what has taken place in the past. The competence of management in administering the enterprise in the years to come can most readily be forecast by examining the record of prior years.

Financial Versus Management Accounting

[9]　A distinction is conventionally made between financial accounting and management accounting. Financial accounting is concerned with reports to parties external to the organization. Management accounting pertains to financial data to be used within the organization.

[10]　Financial accounting focuses primarily on providing information to investors and potential investors. In reporting to outsiders, organizations must adhere to "generally accepted" accounting principles. These principles represent a combination of pronouncements by rule-making authorities and long-standing traditions. They help to assure that the reports are comparable to those of other organizations, that they are consistent over time, and that they are not deliberately false or misleading.

[11]　Management accounting serves the information requirement of insiders—directors, managers, and employees. It provides the information needed to establish the objectives of the organization, to develop the strategies and plans to fulfill those objectives, to administer and control the day-to-day activities of the organization, and to evaluate periodically the success that the organization is having in fulfilling its objectives.④ When it issues reports to insiders, an organization need not satisfy externally imposed standards or adhere to specified accounting principles.

New Words and Expressions

accounting [ə'kauntiŋ]	n.	会计学；会计
summarization [sʌmərai'zeiʃən]	n.	概要，概述
presumably * [pri'zju:məbli]	ad.	大概，可能
corporate * ['kɔ:pərit]	a.	社团的，法人的，共同的
cognizant ['kɔgnizənt]	a.	认识的，知晓的
allocate ['æləkeit]	v.	把（物质，资金等）划归，分配
free enterprise		（企业的）自由经营
subsidize ['sʌbsidaiz]	v.	资助，津贴，给……补助金
entity ['eititi]	n.	实体，统一体
subunit [sub'ju:nit]	n.	下属单位
custodianship [kʌs'təudjənʃip]	n.	保管人的责任，保管人的资格
entrust (to) [in'trust]	v.	托管，委托
score [skɔ:]	n.	帐目；根据；理由
creditor ['kredit]	n.	债权人；贷方，贷项
competence ['kɔmpitəns]	n.	能力，胜任，资格
administer [əd'minist]	vt.	管理，支配；执行，实施
outsider ['aut'saidə]	n.	局外人，外人，外行
adhere to		固守，忠于，坚持
pronouncement [prə'naunsmənt]	n.	见解，表态，声明
comparable * ['kɔmpərəble]	a.	可比较的，类似的
deliberately [di'libəreitli]	ad.	故意地，蓄意地
insider ['insaidə]	n.	内部人，局内人，知情人

Notes

①本句中"be aware of"和"be cognizant of"是并列谓语，共用一个"should"。其中"but equally important"是插入语。

②本句中"be it capitalism or socialism"是省略了"whether"的让步状语从句。(=whether it be capitalism or socialism)，因为当让步状语从句省略whether时，谓语用原形动词（一般为"be"）；主语，谓语须颠倒. 主句中的"as to .... be invested"是介词短语作定语修饰"decisions"，而"contained in financial statements"是过去分词短语作定语修饰"information"。

③本句中"required to make ... financial resources"是过去分词短语作定语修饰"information"。"as to where ... financial resources"是介词短语作定语修饰"decisions"

④本句中"needed to establish... ; to develop ..., to administer ... ; to evaluate ..."都是

过去分词短语作定语，修饰 information。而 "to fulfill those objectives" 是不定式短语作 "strategies and plans" 的定语。

Exercises

Reading Comprehension

Ⅰ. Choose the best answer.

1. Having read this text, you are sure to _____.
   A. be a qualified manager
   B. become a wise investor
   C. be good at accounting
   D. learn some knowledge and skills which enable you to make full use of accounting information

2. The author says that accounting is a dynamic discipline, he probably means _____.
   A. that accounting is always done by some movable means
   B. that accounting discipline is very powerful
   C. that in this discipline, new principles and procedures are frequently changing and developing
   D. that there are periodic changes in economic values measured by accounting

3. Allocation of social resources is attempted to _____.
   A. invest capital
   B. make good and reasonable use of resources
   C. decide whom to subsidize
   D. make loan decisions

4. Within an organization, management involves _____.
   A. controling human and material resources
   B. profit and nonprofit entities
   C. products and subunits
   D. productive functions

5. The third purpose served by accounting information, mentioned in the passage, is _____.
   A. to report on the custodianship of resources
   B. to entrust resources to professional managers and governmental officials
   C. to evaluate people's performance in office
   D. to put the custodianship under people's supervision

Ⅱ. Say whether the following statements are True (T) or False (F) according to the text.

(   ) 1. The purpose of the text is to tell managers and investors how to plan, control and evaluate the activities of the organizations.

( ) 2. Accounting information measures and communicates with varieties of financial data.

( ) 3. Those who try to get information from financial statements are mainly concerned with how well the enterprise will perform in the future.

( ) 4. Financial accounting differs from management accounting in its function.

( ) 5. Management accounting must exactly follow the "generally accepted accountingprinciples, but financial accounting not necessarily does.

Vocabulary

I. Match the words in Column A with their corresponding definitions in Column B.

A	B
1. presumably	a. support firmly
2. allocate	b. probably
3. creditor	c. control or look after (esp. business affairs)
4. adhere	d. divid and give as share
5. administer	e. a person to whom money is owed

II. Complete the following sentences with the words given below. Change the form if necessary.

> enterprise, accounting, comparable, periodic, subsidize

1. Ideally, financial reports of one enterprise should be readily _____ with those of the others.
2. Accountants are concerned with the determination of _____ changes in economic values.
3. Other groups of users such as creditors, employees, may also be able to obtain a wealth of information from the _____ reports.
4. Will the _____ be able to meet the wage demands of its employees?
5. In every western country the state _____ education, housing and health provision.

Reading Material A

Standards

Relevancy

If information provided by the accountant is to be useful, then, above all, it must be relevant—it must bear upon or be associated directly with the decision sit is designed to facilitate. ① unfortunately, what is relevant for one group of financial statement users may not be relevant for another. As a result there is no such thing as "all-purpose" financial statements. Data that may be useful for one type of decision may be useless—or highly misleading—for another. What might be useful to an investor might mislead a manager.

The average cost per unit would be the relevant cost for the determination of overall income to be reported to investors. But for a management decision as to whether or not to accept the offer of the government, the relevant cost would be the incremental or marginal cost—the cost of producing the additional units required for the government contract. ②

Objectivity

Accounting information should, ideally, be objective and verifiable. Qualified individuals working independently of one another should be able, upon examination of the same data or-records, to derive similar measures or reach similar conclusions. Insofar as possible information contained in financial reports should not depend on the subjective judgments of the individual accountant who prepared it.

Herein lies a catch. ③ Information that is most objective may not be relevant to many decisions, and that which is most relevant may not be objective. ④

One of the central themes of this text is that a great many accounting issues can be attributable to the conflict between the objectives of relevance and objectivity. Accountants are continually faced with situations in which they must trade the realization of one goal for that of the other.

Uniformity

Accounting practices should be uniform both within and among corporations or other organizations. Ideally, financial reports of one enterprise should be readily comparable with those of another. In practice, the goal of comparability has not yet been achieved. Such failure can be ascribed to at least two causes. First, until recently both the professional accounting societies and the government agencies responsible for establishing accounting principles and maintaining accounting standards have allowed individual companies a relatively free hand in selecting among alternative accounting practices.⑤ Even today, for example, some firms within the same industry will assume that goods purchased first are sold first, while others will assume that goods purchased last are sold first. Second, the task of prescribing uniform principles that would be appropriate for all companies—or even those within a specific industry—is one that is easier to write about than to accomplish. In the last several decades the range and complexity of business transactions have increased enormously. Accounting procedures designed to account for one type of transaction may be highly inappropriate for a slightly different transaction or even an identical transaction that takes place under slightly differing circumstances.

Consistency

For a reader to compare performance in one period with that in another, financial statements must be based on accounting practices that are consistent over time. Thus, although different firms may make differing assumptions pertaining to the flow of goods, The same firm would ordinarily be expected to base its financial reports on the same assumptions from one year to the next. "A foolish consistency," Emerson pointed out, however, "is the hobgoblin of little minds." In an era of a rapidly changing business environment, accounting practice must necessarily change also. Hence, over a number of years, some degree of consistency must be sacrificed in order for accounting to achieve its other objectives.

Notes

①要使会计所提供的资料起作用，那么，这些资料首先必须具有相关性。即这些资料必须与决策直接有关，而且它们的目的是为了促进决策的制定。
②但是对于一个是否接受政府提出的单位成本的管理决策来说，这种相关成本应是增支成本或边际成本——即产生与政府所需要的单位件数的成本。
③这里"catch"是名词，意思是"使人难以理解的问题"。
④"and that which is …"中的"that"代替的是"information"那种最具客观性的资料可能会与许多决策无关，而那些与决策相关的资料又可能是不客观的。
⑤首先，直至今日，专业会计学会及那些负责制定会计原则和维护会计标准的政府机构都一直允许各公司相对地选用那些可供选择的会计实务。

Reading Material B

Nonstandards

Laymen place far greater faith in financial statements than is generally warranted. It is essential, therefore, that the limitations of financial statements be clearly understood.

not accurate

Financial statements are not accurate. This is as true if amounts are carried out to the penny as if they are rounded off to the hundreds or, in the case of many published reports, to the thousands of dollars. ① Accounting statements are necessarily based on estimates; estimates are inherently inaccurate.

not sole measure of performance

Financial data cannot be used as the sole measure of managerial accomplishment. Financial statements of private enterprises generally focus on profit or income. But profit is by no means a comprehensive measure of performance. Profit tells only a small part of the annual story of a business. Profit for a period of one year can readily be manipulated in order to make an enterprise "look good." To the extent that a manager knows that he will be evaluated on the basis of income for a given single year he can readily increase reported profit by postponing maintenance and nonessential repairs, cutting back on advertising and research and development costs, and reducing the quality of products or services. ② The negative impact of such actions is unlikely to be reflected in reported profits until subsequent years.

But profit, even over a longer period of time, may be only a poor indication of management performance. Profit, after all, can be influenced by factors over which a manager has little control. As long as profits are influenced to a considerable extent by forces beyond management control net income by itself may be an inappropriate criterion for management evaluation.

Moreover, managers have goals in addition to that of maximizing profit. Many managers would include among their goals improving the environment surrounding company plants; increasing the economic, social, physical, and mental well-being of employees; and increasing the number of minority employees on the corporate payroll. ③ Accountants do not purport that the extent to which such objectives have been achieved is given recognition in conventional financial statements.

not neutral

Financial statements are not neutral. It is often said that accounting information must be unbiased——that accountants should be disinterested umpires who "call'em like they see'em." Accountants may indeed attempt to use an unbiased measuring device when reporting on economic events. But value judgments enter into the measurement process as accountants determine what to measure. Accountants measure income as conventionally defined: revenues less expenses. But they include in their measurements only selected revenues and expenses. They do not, for example, include in their financial reports costs of "externalities," such as water or air pollution, employee injuries, or discriminatory hiring practices. Similarly, they fail to give recognition to the benefits received by their efforts to clean up the environment, improve community welfare, and eliminate safety hazards. Indeed several firms, on an experimental basis, have prepared "social" income statements and balance sheets which are based on nonconventional judgments as to what revenues and costs should be measured and reported upon.④

not designed to minimize taxes

The primary criterion by which the adequacy of financial statements should be judged is not whether they minimize the tax liability of the reporting business entity. In the course of this text, numerous alternative accounting procedures will be presented and evaluated. The merits of the alternatives will normally be considered in terms of their objectivity and their relevance to the users of the financial information. Sometimes, unfortunately, a company's choice among alternatives is motivated primarily by income tax considerations, and as a consequence its financial reports are both less objective and less useful to stockholders and potential investors than they might otherwise be.

That is not to say that managers and accountants should not carry out a firm's activities so as to pay the least amount of taxes legally permissible.

Notes

①把金融报表中的总数精确到分与精确到百元或像许多已公布的（金融）报告中把总数精确到千元一样都是不精确的。
②到了经理意识到将要根据某一年度的收入对他进行评估的时候，他很可能会通过延缓设备的维护和不必要的修理；削减广告，研究及开发费用；并降低产品和服务质量等手段，从而轻易地提高他的帐面利润。
③经理们的众多目标中主要包括：改善公司各工厂周围的环境；提高雇员们的经济，社会，物质和精神待遇；在公司工资名单上增加少数民族雇员的人数。
④实际上，有几家公司在实验基础上已制出了"社会"收益报表和资产负债表。这些报表是在对什么样的收益和支出应该加以计算和报告等方面作出非常规的判断的基础上制定出来的。

UNIT TWELVE

Text   Contractor's Duties

Extension of time

[1]   The contractor's duties are rules which the contractor must follow:

[2]   As soon as the contractor thinks he is being delayed or is likely to be delayed in the future, he must immediately notify you in writing. Verbal notification or notification minuted in agreed site meeting minutes is not sufficient.① The notice must include the reasons for the delay and state, in his opinion, which if any of the causes of the delay is a relevant event.②

[3]   As soon as possible, the contractor must give details of the expected results of the relevant events.

[4]   As soon as possible, the contractor must estimate the extent of the expected delay beyond the contract completion date. He must note the effect of each relevant event separately, stating whether or not the delays will be concurrent. If he estimates that there will be no overall delay to the contract completion date, he must so inform you.

[5]   If the contractor makes any reference to a nominated subcontractor, he must send a copy of the written notice, particulars and estimate of delay to the nominated sub-contractor concerned.

[6]   The contractor must give you further notices to update the particulars of delay and estimate of the effect on the completion date from time to time as necessary or in order to comply with your requests. He must send a copy of each such further notice to any nominated sub-contractors who received a copy of the first notice.

[7]   The contractor has a continuing obligation to notify delays throughout the contract period and until the works have reached practical completion. Failure to do so will put him in breach of the terms of the contract, quite apart from seriously affecting his chances of obtaining any extension of time.

[8]   It is in the contractor's own interests to present all the information he has. He must carefully document his notices to you and answer any requests for further information promptly. In effect, the contractor has to argue his case.

[9]   Besides providing written notices to you, the contractor has two further duties.

[10]   He must constantly use his best endeavours to prevent delay in progress and prevent or reduce any effect upon the completion date. This does not mean that he should spend money to make up any delay but that he should be sure that he is proceeding diligently.③ Thus, if any part of the delay is his own fault, it can be interpreted as a lack of endeavour on his part, depending upon the circumstances.

[11]   He must do everything that you reasonably require to proceed with the works. It is not reasonable for you to require the contractor to spend additional money without recompense to catch up on delays but, with this proviso, the contractor's clear duty is to follow your instructions with regard to progress.

[12]   These two duties are closely connected. If the employer requires and authorises acceleration measures together with appropriate payment, there is a duty upon the contractor to carry them out.

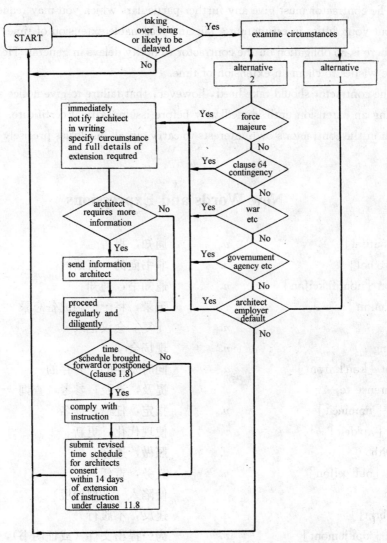

Flow chart 12-1   Contractor's duties in claiming an extension of time under ACA82

[13]   There are two sets of provisions for extensions of time—alternative 1 and altenative 2. The grounds for extension are different (alternative 2 is broader) but the contractor's duties are the same in each case. They are shown in flow chart 12-1. The contract lays down precise rules which the contractor must follow:

[14]　As soon as the contractor thinks he is being delayed or is likely to be delayed in the future and, as a result, the taking-over of the works on the due date will be prevented, he must immediately notify you in writing. It must be a specific notice; minutes of site meetings are not sufficient.

[15]　The notice must specify the circumstances and give full and detailed particulars of the extension of time to which he considers he is entitled.④ The information must be as full and clear as possible.

[16]　The contractor must give any further particulars which you may request to enable you to carry out your duties in estimating a fair and reasonable extension of time.

[17]　There is no obligation on the contractor to notify delays in general. He need only notify them if he wishes to claim an extension of time.

[18]　The contractor should take heed, however, that failure to give notice allows you to delay granting an extension until immediately before issuing a final certificate. It is, therefore, very much in the contractor's own interests to carry out all his duties precisely and at the proper time.

New Words and Expressions

notify ['nəutifai]	v.	通知，报告
verbal ['və:bəl]	a.	非书面的，言语的
notification [nəutifi'keiʃən]	n.	通知书，通知
minute ['minit]	v.	记录，将……制成备忘录
	n.	〔复〕会议记录
site meeting	n.	现场会
concurrent [kən'kʌrənt]	a.	同时发生的，并存的
make reference to		提及，涉及；参考，查询
nominate ['nɔmineit]	v.	指定，任命，提名
update * [ʌp'deit]	v.	使现代化，更新
comply with	v.	照做，遵守
obligation [ɔbli'geiʃən]	n.	义务，责任
put... in		使陷入（某种处境）
breach ['bri:tʃ]	n.	违反，不履行
document ['dɔkjumənt]	v.	为…提出文件（或证明书），用文件说明
in progress	ad.	在进行中，在发展中
endeavo (u) r [in'devə]	v.	努力，尽力
	v.	努力，尽力，力图
make/use one's best endeavors		尽最大努力
recompense ['rekəmpens]	n.	报酬，报答；赔偿，补偿
proviso [prə'vaisəu]	n.	限定性条款，附文，（附带）条件

104

| authorize, —ise [ˈɔːθəraiz] | n. | 批准，允许，认可；授权，委任 |
| take head | | 注意，提防，留意 |

Notes

① 句中"minuted in agreed... minutes"是过去分词短语作定语，修饰 notification。

② 本句中"if any"是一个插入语，意为"如果有""果真有"，相当于"if there is any at all"。"which"在这里是连接代词，引导的是 state 的宾语从句。

③ 句中第一个 that 引导的从句"that he should... any delay"和第二个 that 引导的从句"that he should be... proceeding diligently"都是动词 mean 的宾语从句。be sure 后跟 that 从句表示"一定要做到……"。

④ 句中"to which he... is entitled"是一个限制性定语从句，修饰"extension of time"，"entitle to"意为"给……权利或资格"，在从句中用的是被动语态。

Exercises

Reading Comprehension

Ⅰ. Choose the best answer.

1. In the third paragraph, the sentence "... the expected results of the relevant events" refers to _____.

   A. the anticipated consequences due to various causes of the delay

   B. the possible results of the events concerned

   C. what would happen as far as the relevant events are concerned

   D. the results being looked forward to by the relevant events

2. When the author says "... delay beyond the contract completion date" in paragraph 4, he probably implies _____.

   A. the delay of the starting date

   B. the delay of some individual stage

   C. the delay of the provision of wages

   D. both a and b

3. What does the phrase "make reference to" in paragraph 5 mean according to the context?

   A. say something for the reference

   B. make somebody sure of the reference

   C. mention

   D. come to talking about

4. In paragraph 6, "He must send a copy of each such further notice ... the first notice.",

here "the first notice " suggests _____.

A. the notice written at first

B. the first—class quality in writing

C. the written notice of particulars and estimate of the delay

D. none of the above

5. Which of the following can substitute for "take heed " in the last paragraph?

A. take advantage

B. take note

C. take time

D. take it easy

II. Say whether the following statements are True (T) or False (F) according to the text.

(   ) 1. If any delay is likely to happen, written notification is necessary.

(   ) 2. It's unnecessary for the contractor to keep notifying delays all the time until thecompletion of the construction.

(   ) 3. The first of the two further duties is that the contractor must always minimize the delay and any effect on the completion date by all means.

(   ) 4. The second of the two further duties is that the contractor must do his best to work.

(   ) 5. From flow chart 12-1, it can be concluded that alternatives 1 and 2 are the same as to the duties upon the contractor.

Vocabulary

I. Match the words in Column A with their corresponding definitions in Column B.

A	B
1. update	a. give power to
2. endeavor	b. make more modern
3. authorise	c. make payment to
4. concurrent	d. an effort; attempt
5. recompense	e. existing or happening at the same time

II. Complete the following sentences with some of the words listed below. Change the form if necessary.

> notify, specify, estimate,
> provision, obligation

1. Construction contracts contain numerous _____ that establish an owner's right to obtain quality work.

2. When the contractor thinks the completion date is likely to be delayed, he must _____ the architect in writing.

3. I should be pleased to receive your _____ of the adjustment to the contract sum which you require.

4. There is no express _____ for the contractor to provide further particulars at the architect's request.

5. If the contractor wishes to claim under the provisions of clause 53, he must _____ the circumstance in the notice and state that he is entitled to an increase in the contract sum thereby.

Reading Material A

Who Should Be Responsible for Defective Work?

Construction contracts contain numerous provisions that establish an owner's right to obtain quality work. These provisions ensure that the construction strictly conforms to the contract specifications by allowing the owner to inspect the work at reasonable intervals during construction.[1]

The owner can uncover and expose work—such as underground piping—which the owner believes may be defective.[2] The contractor also has a great interest in these provisions, since such provisions define the steps required for acceptance of the work.

Once the owner has accepted a construction project, he can't require the contractor to correct defects in the work—unless the defects are hidden or the acceptance was obtained by fraudulent means.[3] Usually, there is a great deal of argument on construction projects as to exactly when acceptance has occurred.

An example of this is demonstrated through the recent case between the City of Gering and the Patricia G. Smith company. This case involved the construction of a gravity flow sewer system for the city. Construction was divided into four interconnected parts. Each part was designed by the same engineer, and was separately bid upon and constructed by different contractors.

Smith, the contractor, completed the construction of the fourth part of the project in November 1976. One mouth later the engineer signed a certificate of completion stating that the project had been fully completed according to the terms of the contract. The certificate also recommended that the work be accepted by the owner. The City of Gering accepted Smith's work based upon the engineer's certificate.

After the acceptance, the city complained to the contractor that a sag existed in one of the lines. When the contractor failed to fix the line, the city hired another contractor to perform the work and brought suit against Smith. The lower court awarded a $26,000 judgment against Smith. This judgment was appealed by both Smith and the city. (The city wanted a higher award.) On appeal, the Supreme Court reversed the award.

The testimony showed that at least one member of the engineering firm working on the project knew that a sag existed in the lines before the firm signed its certificate of completion. This engineer said that his firm had surveyed the entire project and suggested the sagging pipe be elevated at this point.④

The Supreme Court said that the City of Gering did nothing about the engineer's suggestion and accepted the project as finished, so the Smith Company did not have to repair the defect. Also, there was no evidence of fraud. The certificate of completion had the contractual purpose of telling both the city and the contractor that the work was done properly.⑤ If the city intended to object to the work because of the sag, it had to do so before accepting it.

The City of Gering case demonstrates the care which must be taken prior to signing a certificate accepting a project. Courts will often be practical in analyzing the actions of the parties and determining whether a contractor should bear additional costs in correcting defective work. In the City of Gering decision the contractor successfully passed all of requirements established by the contract for acceptance—including obtaining the recommendation by the engineer. The risks of defects found after this time were shifted to the owner.

Notes

①这些条款保证：施工要严格地遵守合同技术要求。采取的办法是，允许业主在施工的适当时候，检查工程状况。
②业主认为可能有缺陷的工程——象下水道这样的工程，他可以揭开覆盖层，使工程的面目显露出来。
③业主一旦验收了一项工程，他就不能再要求承包人对工程中的质量问题承担返修责任——除非这类工程的缺陷被隐瞒了，或采用欺骗手段通过了验收手续。
④这位工程师说，公司检查过整个工程，并建议把管道下陷的地方垫高。
⑤竣工证书具有合同效力，它告知盖林市和承包人双方：这项工程已全部完工。

Reading Material B

The Weather's Effect on Performance of Construction Contracts

It is no secret—weather indirectly affects the decisions a contractor must make in planning the construction of a project. Equipment, manpower and order of construction activities are all affected by the weather. It also directly affects one of the most critical parts of construction -- timely contract completion. Because financial penalties are often imposed for late completion, contractors must be able to correctly predict weather conditions before the bid to ensure job profitability. [1]

Fortunately, construction contractors do not bear all the risk for weather conditions that might affect contract completion. If the project is delayed because of weather, a contractor will generally not be penalized. This common law theory is decided from the fact that weather is an "Act of God" for which neither side should be penalized. [2]

It is difficult to prove that completion is impossible due to weather conditions. A general understanding between the contractor and the owner is not specific enough. Therefore, the standard in the construction industry is for the parties to include in the contract a section about delays due to weather. [3] A recent example—the Wallace case shows what weather conditions justify a time extension.

In the Wallace case the contractor agreed to replace two roofs on warehouses in Albany Georgia. The contract contained a financial penalty for each day of unexcused delay beyond the contract completion date unless such delays were caused by unforeseen causes beyond the contractor's control, such as unusually severe weather. [4] The contract was completed 124 days after the scheduled date. The Armed Services Board of Contract Appeals was called upon to determine whether the delay was excusable because of weather conditions. The board found that the weather was not so severe as to excuse the contractor.

The contractor argued that bad weather caused the delay. The contractor said that work would not be done when the air temperature was below 30 degrees Fahrenheit and there was ice, frost, surface moisture or visible dampness on the roof deck.

The Government used weather data from the previous five year averages for temperature and moisture to calculate a schedule for finishing the work. The Government demonstrated that the contractor should have expected 90 days of precipitation and 17 days of cold weather. The contractor was proven to be 17 days behind schedule after allowing for the predictable 107 days of bad weather.

The Board accepted the Government's position for several reasons. First, uncontested Government testimony demonstrated that only 4 days were actually lost due to cold weather and only 38 complete and 22 partial working days were lost due to rain. Thus, the contractor's work was not very much affected by the weather. The Board agreed that the contractor should have expected such delays. Second, testimony demonstrated that the delay was caused by material shortages, labor problems and improper scheduling. Finally, the contractor did not give evidence to show expected weather delays when bidding.

Contractors should not only prove that weather conditions were more severe than an historical average, but that they were actually delayed by such weather. [5] On the one hand, contractors benefit from generous time extensions. They cannot be penalized for late work, as long as the work is completed before the extension expires. On the other hand, the owner can legally demand payment from the contractor once the deadline passes.

Notes

①由于工程延期,常常迫使承包商支付违约金,因此,承包商必须在投标以前,能正确无误地预测天气条件的多种情况,以确保工程项目有利可图。

②这种不成文的法律理论是根据这样的事实决定的:即天气是一种不可抗拒的力量,对此,任何一方都不该受罚。

③所以,建筑行业的惯常做法是:双方合同应含因天气原因而延误工期的条款。

④该合同有一条罚款条文:在合同竣工期满以后,凡未能按合同履行的无理延误,要逐日予以罚款,除非这种延误是由承包商无法控制、又难以预测的原因引起的,例如非同寻常的恶劣天气。

⑤承包商不仅应该证实天气条件要比历史上的平均天气状况更为恶劣,而且还应该证实他们确实是由于这种恶劣天气而造成了工期的延误。

UNIT THIRTEEN

Text Plan Shape

[1]　The shape of a building has an important effect on cost. As a general rule the simpler the shape of the building the lower will be its unit cost. As a building becomes longer and narrower or its outline is made more complicated and irregular, so the perimeter/floor area ratio will increase, accompanied by a higher unit cost.① The significance of perimeter/floor area relationships will be considered in more detail in the unit. An irregular outline will also result in increased costs for other reasons: setting out, siteworks and drainage work are all likely to be more complicated and more expensive. The additional costs do not finish there as brickwork and roofing will also be more costly due to the work being more complicated. It is important that both architect and client are aware of the probable additional costs arising from comparatively small changes in the shape of a building.

[2]　Although the simplest plan shape, that is, a square building, will be the most economical to construct it would not always be a practicable proposition.② In dwellings, smaller offices, schools and hospitals considerable importance is attached to the desirability of securing adequate natural daylighting to most parts of the buildings. A large, square structure would contain areas in the centre of the building which would be deficient in natural lighting. Difficulties could also arise in the planning and internal layout of the accommodation. Hence, although a rectangular shaped building would be more expensive than a square one with the same floor area because of the smaller perimeter/floor area ratio, nevertheless practical or functional aspects, and possibly aesthetic ones in addition, may dictate the provision of a rectangular building.③

[3]　Certain types of building present their own peculiar problems which in their turn may dictate the form and shape of the building. For instance hotels, for visual reasons, to provide guests with good views and the advertising effect of a prominent building on the skyline, need to be tall. The shape and floor area are closely related to the most economic bedroom per floor ratio and this is generally in the range of forty to fifty. This dictates a tall slab rather than a tower. Slender towers are aesthetically very desirable but their relatively poor ratio of usable to gross floor area often renders them prohibitively expensive.

[4]　There are occasions when the site itself will dictate the form or shape of the building. In some cases the designer may feel obliged to advise the building client to purchase additional land, where this is practicable, to make the development a more economical proposition. It may be worthwhile to underutilise an awkwardly shaped site in order to secure a regularly shaped and more economical building. Where a strip form of development of possibly eight to ten storeys in height is involved, means of escape considerations alone may dictate the optimum length of building to secure the maximum net to gross floor area relationship.

[5]　　The shape of a building may also be influenced by the manner in which it is going to be used. For instance, in factory buildings the determining factors may be co-ordination of manufacturing processes and the form of the machines and finished products. In schools, dwellings and hospitals, and to a more limited extent in offices, shape is influenced considerably by the need to obtain natural lighting. Where the majority of rooms are to rely on natural lighting in daylight hours, the depth of the building is thereby restricted. Otherwise it is necessary to compensate for the increase in depth of building by installing taller windows which may compel increased storey heights. The aim in these circumstances should be to secure an ideal balanced solution which takes into account both the lighting factor and the constructional costs. Deeper rooms result in reduced perimeter/floor area ratios with a subsequent reduction in construction, maintenance and heating costs, but these savings may be offset by increased lighting costs. With taller rooms the conditions are reversed. Where a high density of rooms is required, the use of an external wall as a boundary to a room may compensate for the amount of partitioning that would otherwise be required.④ It is, therefore sometimes preferable to elongate the building, so that rooms can be entered from either side of a spinal corridor rather than having a deep building with a complex network of corridors to give access to all rooms, together with the possible need for artificial ventilation to internal rooms.⑤

New Words and Expressions

perimeter [pə'rimitə]	n.	周长，周边
setting out		设计；装饰，布置
drainage ['dreinidʒ]	n.	排水（设备）下水道
brickwork ['brikwə:k]	n.	砌砖；砖房，砖瓦工
roofing ['ru:fiŋ]	n.	屋面工程
practicable * ['præktikəbl]	a.	能实行的，行得通的
proposition * [ˌprɔpə'ziʃən]	n.	提议；主张
desirability [diˌzaiərə'biliti]	n.	可取之处；好处，优点
deficient [di'fiʃənt]	a.	不足的；缺乏的
rectangular * [rek'tæŋgjulə]	a.	长方形的，矩形的
aesthetic [i:s'θetik]	a.	美学的；美的，艺术的
slab * [slæb]	n.	平板；厚片，厚板
prohibitively * [prə'hibitivli]	ad.	…得令人不敢问津
underutilise [ˌʌndə'ju:tilaiz]	v.	浪费地使用；对…未充分利用
compensate for *		补偿
offset * ['ɔ:fset]	v.	抵销；弥补
partition * [pɑ:'tiʃən]	v.	分开，隔开；划分
elongate * ['i:lɔŋgeit]	v.	（使）延长；拉长

spinal ['spainl]   a.   脊柱的；脊髓的

Notes

① 这是一个"as…, so…"结构的复合句，意为"随着……，也就……"。
② 该句是一个复合句，主句为"it would not always be a practicable proposition"；"that is a square building"为插入语，进一步说明"the simplest plan shape"。
③ 该句是一个复合句，主要结构为"although…, nevertheless…"，其中"because of"引起的介词短语说明"a square one"。
④ "other wise"意为"要不然；否则"，在该句中意为"如果不把外墙作为房间的墙壁……"。
⑤ 句中"with"和"together with"引起的部分作定语，修饰"a deep building"，其中词组"together with"意为"加之，连同"，另一词组"to give access to"即"接近；给……提供通道，通向"，在句中作定语，修饰"corridors"。

Exercises

Reading Comprehension

Ⅰ. Choose the best answer.

1. It can be inferred from the text that
    A. a rectangular shaped building has a smaller perimeter/floor area ratio.
    B. a large square building needs extra lighting systems.
    C. a rectangular building is preferable in any case.
    D. a tower provides guests with better views.
2. Why does the author mention "a strip form of development" in Paragraph 4?
    A. To advise the client to buy more land
    B. To dictate the provision of a rectangular building
    C. To illustrate the variety of lengths of buildings
    D. To give an example of an irregular site which can be used for a regularly shaped and more economical building
3. Why should hotels be tall?
    A. To draw attention
    B. To dwarf surrounding buildings
    C. To provide billboards
    D. to add colour to the sky
4. In designing factory buildings, which of the following should be considered first?
    A. The provision of natural lighting

B. Artificial ventilation to internal rooms
C. Aesthetic aspects
D. Manufacturing processes and forms of facilities and final products

5. The author implies that taller rooms are accompanied by
   A. a decrease in construction maintenance and heating costs.
   B. increased depth of the building.
   C. consumption of less electricity.
   D. elongated corridors.

II. Identify main ideas for each paragraph by matching the following ideas with their appropriate paragraph numbers.
1. The site dictates the form of a building.
2. The shape of a building has an important effect on expenses.
3. The way in which the building is going to be used may influence its shape.
4. In terms of shape and form, the peculiar problems with a building must be taken into consideration.
5. A square building, though the most economical to construct, is not always preferable.

Vocabulary

I. Fill in the blanks with the expressions given below.

> slab, storey, offset, layout, unit cost,
> ratio, perimeter, underutilise

1. Increases in the size of buildings usually produce reductions in _____, such as the cost of per square metre of floor area.
2. Block shape and depth influence the proportion of external wall area to floor area and the wall/floor _____ varies a great deal for the most complex plans.
3. One aspect which has to be considered when investigating perimeter/floor area ratios is the adequacy of the natural lighting to the interior of the building and the practicability of the internal _____.
4. The best wall/floor ratio is produced by a circular building, but the saving in quantity of wall is more than _____ by the much bigger cost of circular work over straight.
5. The wall to floor ratio is influenced by the plan shape, plan size and _____ heights.

II. Match the words in Column A with their corresponding definitions in Column B.

A	B
1. partition	a. a suggested (business) offer, arrangement or settlement

2. elongate b. in the shape of a plane four-sided figure with four right angles, esp. with adjacent sides unequal
3. rectangular c. most likely to bring advantage; most favourable
4. proposition d. to make (something) longer
5. optimum e. to divide into two or more parts

Reading Material A

Size of Building

Increases in the size of buildings usually produce reductions in unit cost, such as the cost of per square metre of floor area. The prime reason for this is that oncosts are likely to account for a smaller proportion of total costs with a larger project, or expressed in another way, they do not rise proportionately with increases in the plan size of a building. Certain fixed costs such as the transportation, erection and dismantling of site buildings and compounds for storage of materials and components, temporary water supply arrangements and the provision of temporary roads, may not vary, appreciably with an extension of the size of job and will accordingly constitute a reduced proportion of total costs on a larger project. A larger project is often less costly to build as the wall/floor ratio reduces, rooms tend to be larger with a proportional reduction in the quantity of internal partitions, decorations, skirtings, etc., and there may also be a proportional reduction in the extra cost of windows and doors over walls.① With high rise buildings a cost advantage may accrue due to lifts serving a larger floor area and greater number of occupants with an increased plan area.②

An example will serve to illustrate the cost advantage in lift provision by increasing the area on each floor of multistorey blocks of flats and offices. A six-storey block of offices built in the East Midlands in 1982 has 360 m² of floor area on each floor and the six floors are served by two passenger lifts. The total cost of the project of £928000 is equivalent to £430/m² of floor area and the lifts cost £54000 and are equivalent to £25/m² of floor area. If the floor area was doubled on each storey the lift provision could remain the same and the cost of lifts would then be reduced to about £12.50/m² of floor area, giving a saving of 3.0 per cent on total building costs.

Another interesting illustration of the effect of size on building costs emanates from a comparison of the costs of two, three and four bedroom houses. Table 13-1 compares the costs of building two, three and four bedroom houses in a local authority scheme in the West Midlands in 1982. The costs per m² of floor area of the three bedroom houses show a 0.9 per cent reduction on the cost of the two-bedroom houses, and the four-bedroom houses show a 6.5 per cent reduction on the three-bedroom, although the cost of siteworks is shown as remaining constant. When the costs are related to the number of occupiers they show much greater reduc-

115

tions, although it must be appreciated that only a small proportion of the larger houses are fully occupied.

Table 13-1 Comparative cost of two-, three-and four-bedroom local authority houses (two-storey) (1982 prices)

	Two-bedroom four-person house	Three-bedroom five-person house	Four-bedroom seven-person house
Floor area (m²)	75.3	85.1	106.5
Superstructure costs (£)	11408	12995	15658
Substructure costs (£)	2099	2426	2800
Siteworks costs (£)	2394	2394	2394
Total costs (£)	15901	17815	20852
Cost/m² (£)	211.17	209.34	195.79
Cost/person (£)	3975	3563	2979

The 1982 unit cost of the additional floor area of a three-bedroom over a two-bedroom house is £195/m² that of a four-bedroom over a three-bedroom house is £142/m² and that of a four-bedroom over a two-bedroom house is £159/m². ③ Admittedly it would not be prudent to attach too much importance to the relationships drawn from the resuits of a single tender; nevertheiess they do serve to indicate the broad pattern.

Notes

① 由于墙周边长与楼面积之比缩小，而且内部间隔、装饰及壁脚板等方面数量的相应减少使得房间增大，加上墙上门窗的额外开销也会相应减少，因此，较大工程建起来通常要节省一些。
② 就高大建筑而言，由于规划面积增大，所以电梯能为更大的楼层面积及更多的用户服务，因此，造价方面的优势就可能增大。
③ 1982年，一套三居室的房子较之两居室所增加的楼层面积的单位造价是每平方米195英镑，一套四居室的房子较之三居室所增加的楼层面积的单位造价是每平方米142英镑，一套四居室的房子较之两居室所增加的楼层面积的单位造价是每平方米159英镑。

Reading Material B

Perimeter/Floor Area Ratios

We have already seen that the plan shape directly conditions the external walls, windows and external doors which together constitute a composite element—the enclosing walls. Different plans can be compared by examining the ratio of enclosing walls to floor area in square metres (known as the wall/floor ratio). The lower the wall/floor ratio, the more economical will be the proposal. The best wall/floor ratio is produced by a circular building, but the saving in quantity of wall is usually more than offset by the much bigger cost of circular work over straight, the increased cost varying between twenty and thirty per cent.[①] The wall to floor ratio is a means of expressing the planning efficiency of a building and is influenced by the plan shape, plan size and storey heights. The ratio is calculated by dividing the external wall area (inclusive of windows and doors) by the gross floor area.

Figure 13-1 shows the outline of two buildings, one of which (building A) is L shaped and the other (building B) has a very irregular outline. Both buildings have an identical floor area on each floor of $244m^2$, and assuming that the buildings are each of two storeys, this gives a total floor area of $488m^2$ for each building. Wall thicknesses have been ignored in this example to simplify the calculations. The length of enclosing wall in building A amounts to 70m while that in building B totals 100m—an increase of forty-three per cent. Assuming that the height of the walling is 6m—the areas of enclosing walls are $420m^2$ for building A and $600m^2$ for building B and the wall/floor ratios are

$$\text{building A} = 420/488 = 0.86$$
$$\text{building B} = 600/488 = 1.23$$

Building B is very uneconomical with a much greater area of enclosing walls than A. It should be borne in mind that the perimeter cost of a building can be in the order of twenty to thirty per cent of total cost and an external wall can be two to four times as expensive as an internal partition. In this example building B is likely to be at least ten per cent more expensive than building A on account of the much increased perimeter costs.

With traditional construction, the cost of the structure—enclosing walls, windows, roof and floors—increases steadily with an extension of the frontage. As a result wider frontage houses are more expensive than those of narrower frontage with similar floor area.

Graphs produced by the National Building Agency show that the narrow frontage house becomes relatively cheaper as the length of terrace increases, with costs falling moresharply, than with the medium and wide frontage houses.[②] Where both narrow and wide frontage houses and short and long terraces are required, it is more economical to use wide frontage houses in the short terraces and the narrow frontage houses in the long ones.

Another aspect which has to be considered when investigating perimeter/floor area ratios is the adequacy of the natural lighting to the interior of the building and the practicability of the internal layout. By reducing the frontage and increasing the depth of a building the amount of natural light reaching the innermost parts will be reduced and may result in increased operating costs through higher artificial lighting charges. A deeper building may also result in wasteful and inconveniently shaped rooms such as long cubicles housing WCs. Thinner walls will also provide greater floor area for the same length of enclosing wall.

Many blocks of flats are rectangular in plan shape, although some are U, L, Y or T shaped. Block shape and depth influence the proportion of external wall area to floor area and

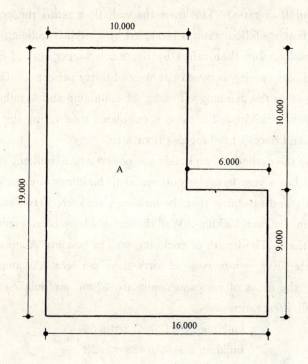

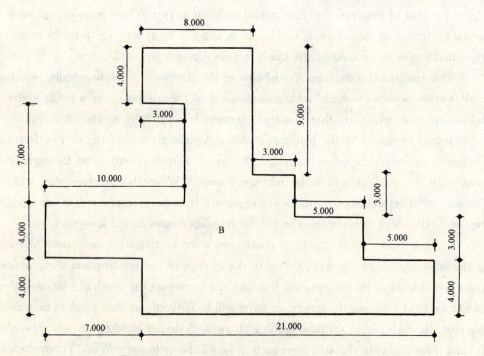

Figure 13-1 Perimeter/floor area ratios

the wall/floor ratio varies from about 1.40 for the most complex plans to 0.60 for the most simple and deepest rectangular plans.

118

Notes

①环形建筑的围墙与楼面面积之比为最佳，但是环形建筑虽然在围墙的数量上节省了，它的建筑费用却比直线型建筑高得多——相抵后它的建筑费用要高出百分之二十到百分之三十。

②国家建设处提供的绘图表明：由于台阶长度增加，造价较明显降低，所以建造一栋正面窄小的房屋要比建造正面不宽不窄和正面宽大的房屋便宜一些。

UNIT FOURTEEN

Text   The Investor's Objectives

[1] The first step in the investment process is to identify the investor's objectives, goals, and constraints. Without this, the feasibility of the investment cannot be determined. In addition to the obvious factors of price appreciation, tax shelter benefits, and financial leverage, we discuss more explicit reasons why individuals or firms invest in real estate. Some investors seek substantial real estate holdings because they feel that real property is more secure, more valuable, and more visible than financial assets. The opportunities for positive cash flows during the holding period of the investment are attractive to many who seek dollar returns. This is reinforced by the relatively small down payment required, the amount of borrowed capital available, as well as the expectation of growth in value of the property when the investor decides to sell. The attractiveness of larger reversion values (selling prices in the future) continues to lure investors, especially given current tax deferment opportunities and recent tax law changes which have lowered capital gains tax rates. ①

[2] Finally, by making periodic debt service payments for amortizing loans, the investor increases his ownership through equity build-up over time. Although this accumulation is slow, the repayment of principal over time will add to the owner's equity, assuming the value of the real estate does not fall. It will supplement increases in equity in addition to property values which may rise over time.

[3] What is the appropriate goal or objective for the investor? Many investors wish to secure the largest income, profit, cash flow, or tax shelter benefits over the life of the holding period. Others are willing to forego these benefits in the hope of realizing large gains from appreciation at the time of sale. Some attempt to measure this performance by using various rate of return measures while others assess performance by measuring increases in the size of their personal assets, or their net worth (or wealth) positions. However, the best goal for each investor is determined by his own objectives, tolerance for risk, and individual tastes and preferences. For many investors, this goal will be the maximization of wealth or net worth.

What is investment?

[4] Early investment analysis distinguished between investment and speculation. Speculation was associated with large risks for great gains or unsecured gambles where the investor used other people's funds to his own advantage. Investment, on the other hand, was viewed as a secure acquisition generally with a steady income and without the use of borrowed funds.

[5] Surprisingly enough, many of these distinctions are still followed today. However, it is difficult to distinguish between speculation and investment. If an individual becomes interested

in purchasing some property for significant financial gain, and he analyzes the property in a particular area to the best of his ability, do we call this individual a speculator rather than an investor? Or if the investor has a very short expected holding period, or if the expected rate of appreciation is relatively high due to growth in the community, or if he believes that future rates of appreciation in property of this type will be high, is this so-called speculator different than other investors? Obviously, the answer is no. The historical distinction placed upon speculation and investment is not useful and, in some cases, is quite unclear.

Risk and return move together

[6]   Risk and return are inseparable. Investment opportunities that promise high rates of return also tend to be high risk. Similarly, those properties that appear to be safer and less risky typically yield less future returns. Given our market economy, the relationship between risk and return must be expected since buyers and sellers in the market are constantly evaluating the effects of changing market conditions on property value.① Changes which have dramatic effects on investments have similar effects on the expected return and/or risk of the projects as viewed by the market participants. Therefore, market prices rise or fall according to expected impacts as a result of the change. Since one cannot get "something for nothing" (without superior information that the rest of the market does not possess!), risk and return move together.

[7]   In a market economy, where risk and return more together, one may expect to find the relationship in equilibrium between risk and required rate of return. Without any risk there still is a return, due to the foregone use of funds during the period of the investment. However, as increasing amounts of return are desired, it would only come with increasing amounts of risk. In this analysis, the investor is free to pick the amount of risk to be undertaken which would then translate into an expected return.

New Words and Expressions

feasibility * [ˌfiːzəˈbiliti]	n.	可行性，可能性
appreciation [əˌpriːʃiˈeiʃən]	n.	涨价，增值；估计
tax shelter		减税
leverage [ˈliːvəridʒ]	n.	杠杆作用；影响，力量
explicit * [iksˈplisit]	a.	显然可见的；明晰的
real estate		房地产，不动产
down payment		定金
lure [ljuə]	v.	诱惑；吸引
deferment [diˈfəːmənt]	n.	迟延；延期
amortize [əˈmɔːtaiz]	v.	分期偿还；转让

equity	['ekwiti]	n.	（押款金额以外的）财产价值；股票；公平，公道
accumulation	[əˌkju:mju'leiʃən]	n.	积累；积聚物
forego	[fɔ:'gəu]	v.	放弃；发生在……之前
maximization	[ˌmæksimai'zeiʃən]	n.	最大限度化
speculation	[ˌspekju'leiʃən]	n.	投机；思索，推测
unsecured	[ˈʌnsiˈkjuəd]	n.	无抵押的，无担保的；没系牢的
gamble	['gæmbl]	n.	投机，冒险；赌博
speculator	['spekjuleitə]	n.	投机者；思索者
inseparable	[in'sepərəbl]	a.	不可分离的
participant *	[pɑ:'tisipənt]	n.	参与者；参加者
equilibrium *	[ˌi:kwi'libriəm]	n.	平衡；均势；不偏不倚

Notes

① "given" 在此作介词，意即 "如果将 …… 考虑在内"。

Exercises

Reading Comprehension

I . choose the best answer.

1. Which of the following conclusions is not supported in the first three paragraphs?

   A. Investors would like to choose real estate investment rather than other alternatives.

   B. Investment in real property is more likely to bring about benefits.

   C. There are various forms of investment.

   D. Investors wish to make as much profit as possible.

2. Traditionally, people believe that

   A. speculators gamble with other people's money.

   B. investment is preferable to speculation.

   C. it is hard to tell the difference between speculation and investment.

   D. it is not of much significance to distinguish between speculation and investment.

3. The author suggests that confidential information about the market will especially benefit the

   A. loaner.

   B. tax payer.

   C. investor.

   D. debtor.

122

4. Which of the following sayings is best illustrated in the last two paragraphs?
   A. You can't eat your cake and have it, too.
   B. No pains, no gains.
   C. Diamond cut diamond.
   D. What one loses on the swings one gets back on the roundabouts.
5. What is the author's attitude toward investment?
   A. Pessimistic
   B. Conservative
   C. Uninterested
   D. Objective

II. Give definitions to the following terms.
   1. equity build-up _____
   2. reversion values _____
   3. equilibrium _____
   4. down payment _____
   5. real estate _____

Vocabulary

I. Fill in the missing words for the following sentences, making use of the given paragraph reference number.
   1. Insurance on our homes, our automobiles. and our lives protects us against some of the most common _____ to which we are exposed. (Para. 4)
   2. Given other factors like inflation protection and financial _____, investments in property appear to be very safe and secure. (Para. 1)
   3. Insurance can be _____ against such hazards as floods, earthquakes, loss from employee theft, burglary, robbery and many other causes. (Para. 5)
   4. The prospect of continued increases in value at rates greater than those on other _____ attracts many individuals or firms to invest in real estate. (Para. 1)
   5. If the investment rate of _____ is greater than the cost of borrowed funds, the investor gets a gain as a result. (Para. 7)

II. Choose the word that is closest in meaning to the underlined part.
   1. The first step in the investment process is to identify the investor's objectives, goals and constraints.
      A. targets   B. motives   C. restrictions   D. intentions
   2. Investors in real estate are attracted by such factors as price appreciation, tax shelter benefits and financial leverage.
      A. rise in value   B. evaluation   C. adaptation   D. judgment
   3. Repaying principal over time will add to the owner's equity.

123

      A. tax   B. leaders   C. money   D. bills

4. Real estate investing allows the investor to make periodic debt service payments for amortizing loans.

    A. retracting   B. deferring   C. paying off   D. offsetting

5. The equity build-up helps the investor refinance the property or use the increased part for additional profits.

    A. equality   B. property value   C. criterion   D. quality

Reading Material A

Risk and Return

Types of Risk

There are many types of risk that an investor must analyze in making an investment. These are:

1. *Market (business) risk.* The possibility that an investment will not generate the level of net income that is expected. Many factors could lead to a decline in net income. In general, shifts in supply and demand cause rents and values to increase or decrease.

2. *Inflation (purchasing power) risk.* The possibility that price increases will be greater than expected and result in a decline in future purchasing power.

3. *Legislative (political) risk.* The possibility that the government will change policy or laws that affect the investment, such as changes n tax laws, zoning ordinances, and other elements of the legal environment.

4. *Financial (borrowing) risk.* The possibility that an investment will not generate sufficient income to cover debt obligations.

The point is that *evaluating risk is as important as evaluating return*. The extent to which investment opportunities exist in the real estate market is the extent to which risk must be evaluated as closely as expected returns.① Investment analysis is the analysis of risk and return for various investment alternatives. As a matter of fact, investing is choosing among market alternatives in order to achieve some financial objective or goal. The basic goal is to maximize the wealth of the investor which involves maximization of property value. The investment decision is the commitment of certain cash outflow in return for risky cash inflows.

Expected, Required, and Actual Rates of Return

To understand investment decision making, it is necessary to differentiate between and define three rates of return: the expected rate, the required rate, and the actual (realized) rate.

The investment decision is made by comparing the expected rate of return to the required rate. The *expected rate* is what the investor forecasts that the investment will yield, based on expectations regarding cash outflows in relation to cash inflows.② For example, suppose that an investor is considering an investment with an outflow of $1,000 and expects to receive $1,100 after one year. The expected rate of return is 10%.

Should the investment be made? To answer this question, the investor must determine the *required rate of return*. Basically, the required rate of return is related to two factors: time and risk. The investor must be compensated for waiting even if there is no risk. The greater the perceived level of risk, the greater the required rate of return. Returning to our example, suppose that the investor decides that a 12% rate of return is required. Should the investment be made? No, because the investor requires 12% and the investment is expected to pay 10%. Because the expected rate is less than the required rate of return, the investment is rejected. On the other hand, if the expected rate is greater than the required rate of return, the investment is accepted. For example, if the required rate is 8% and the expected is 10%, the investment is made.

Now let's extend the example. Suppose that the investment is accepted at an outflow of $1,000, and one year later the investor receives $1,200. Since we know the actual income in this situation, we can calculate the actual (realized) rate of return, which is 20%. In this example, the investor required 8%, expected 10%, and realized 20%.

We can calculate the actual rate of *return* only after the investment is made. It is thus an ex post number, that is, a historical rate.③ We make the decision based on the future. Obviously, the actual rate of return may be less than, greater than, or equal to what we expected. Likewise, the actual rate may be different from the required rate of return.

Notes

①房地产市场投资机会有多大，风险就该以多大的精确程度来估计，就象估计预期收益那样。
②预期收益率是投资者根据对现金流出量和现金流入量的期望值预测出的投资将会带来的收益率。该句中"what"相当于 the rate that，其中 rate 是"yield"的宾语；"that the investment will yield"是"forecasts"的宾语从句。
③因此，这是一个"事后的"数字，即实际收益率。

Reading Material B

Reasons for Investing

There are a number of reasons why investing in real estate is favorable. Each is listed below and briefly discussed separately although many are interrelated.

Investment Security

Historically, many investors have held that since the supply of land is essentially fixed, market demand forces will continuously drive up the value. Therefore, real estate appears to be more secure than other investments since the supply of most others can be expanded. This results in a very secure position for the holder since the risk of loss due to a decline in value is very small or nonexistent. Furthermore, it has been argued that real estate returns by nature appear to be less variable over time and are therefore more predictable. Finally, given other factors like inflation protection and leverage gains, investments in property appear to be very safe and secure.

Available Cash Flows

The prospect of extra money accruing to the investor after all expenses and debts are paid each period (month or year) is an attractive feature of investing in real estate. (After-tax cash flow is defined as net operating income less debt service less income taxes each period.) Cash flow differs from taxable income because deduction of interest payments is permitted for tax purposes and because depreciation allowances are non-cash expenses.

Financial Leverage

Real estate investing allows the investor to borrow a majority of the necessary funds with relatively little cash (or with a low down payment). If the investment rate of return is greater than the cost of borrowed funds, a gain accrues to the investor as a result.

The drawback, of course, is that the leverage gain occurs only as a result of a corresponding increase in the amount of financial risk in the project.

Tax Shelter Benefits

Since depreciation reduces taxable income and does not involve cash outflow, the tax liability will be smaller. Therefore, depreciation allowances enable tax savings.

This is compounded by the provisions that permit investors to use an accelerated method of depreciation. In addition, taxable losses, as a result of depreciation, frequently occur with positive cash flows. The deductions lower taxable income, which reduces tax to zero (or less). If taxable income is negative, these "losses" may offset tax liability from other income.

Property Value Appreciation

Because well-located and well-maintained property in growing communities or choice sites in urban areas have continued to grow in value in real terms, these relative price changes have resulted in large capital gains for property owners. The prospect of continued increases in value at rates greater than those on other assets attracts many investors.

Equqity Position

Since the mortgage instrument typically requires a fixed amount of repayment, the accumulation of equity as a result of satisfying the mortgage over time is called equity build-up. The equity build-up helps the investor refinance the property or use the increased equity for additional projects. This process, called *pyramiding*, and changes in the equity position are of critical concern to the investor.

Inflation Hedge

In essence, future growth in real estate will be advantageous to the investor only if relative prices of real estate exceed expectations about general price level changes. Therefore, as long as real estate values continue to rise at unexpectedly higher rates than predicted, real estate will be attractive to those seeking protection from falling real values due to price erosion.

Portfolio Considerations

If real estate is expected to perform differently than other investments, this may be beneficial for investors. This gain would occur as a result of diversification and therefore, the overall riskiness of the investor's portfolio would be reduced. Indeed, one of the key rules in developing an investment strategy is to remember that, in general, it is not wise to put "all of your eggs in one basket."

Non-economic Reasons

Although market prices should reflect supply and demand pressures including those that result from non-economic factors, some investors argue that real estate appeals to them for aesthetic, social, or political reasons.① Some investors would rather own twelve-flat luxury apartment buildings in the nicest part of the community for the "social" contribution this makes to the commuity.② Others argue that real property investments are more tangible than alternative investments. Finally, some investors satisfy consumption objectives as well as investment goals when choosing certain types of investment. While these objectives may not always appear to be financially sound, they have been included since some investors place positive values on these non-pecuniary benefits.

Notes

①虽然市场价格应当反映供需方面的压力，包括产生于非经济因素方面的压力，但是 有些投资者却争论说，他们对房地产感兴趣是因为审美、社会以及政治方面的原因。

②一些投资者宁愿在社区最好的地段拥有十二层豪华公寓大楼，就是为了给社区作出"社会"贡献。

UNIT FIFTEEN

Text   Contracts (General, Identification of Project, Preparation of Scope)

[1]   A contract has been defined as a promise made between two or more parties which is enforceable by law. A contract is necessary, therefore, to protect both client and contractor.

General

[2]   The objectives of the client and contractor are very different. In general, the former strives to achieve successful completion of the project on time, at minimum cost, whilst the latter's objective is to increase profit. This is a point that many a client misses.

[3]   Several standard conditions of contract exist to facilitate the drawing up of a legal document, to which both parties adhere. Some of these contracts are biased towards the contractor and others towards the client.① In other words, the risk-bearing role is borne by one, or both parties concerned. It is in the interest of the manager to select the best contract that fits the needs of the organisation and the project.②

[4]   With this in view, the following factors must be continually reviewed in relation to the contract:

[5]   1. *Project scope* the extent or area which it covers. Any additions or omissions during the life of the project will increase or decrease the quantity of work involved. Likewise, any changes in design must be scrutinised carefully to establish whether or not they are likely to affect the scope of a project.

[6]   2. *Time*. The scope and time are closely interrelated, and decisions must often be made on the effect of time on the increasing or decreasing scope. If the completion date for a project is critical, then increasing scope will call for an accelerated programme. The extra costs associated with this acceleration must be quantified and an assessment made of the impact these costs will have on the financial aspects, ie, return on investment.③

[7]   3. *Price*. Again, this aspect is closely related to scope and time. Much of the discussion in this unit will centre on the effect of the contract on price, and the various incentives and penalties that can help to keep price steady.

[8]   There are eight essential steps to be taken before placing a contract. These are represented in Figure 15-1.

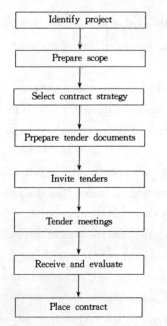

Figure 15-1   Pre-contract stages

The first four stages will now be dealt with in turn.

Identification of project

[9] Project identification is the first step in the chain of events leading up to the placing of a contract. The decisions taken here will have repercussions throughout the pre-contract and administration phases.

[10] Project identification must be closely linked to the organisation's overall aims and objectives. Often a project, selected and worked upon for some considerable time, is discovered to be in conflict with an overall corporate plan.

[11] A marketing function, for example, may predict a rosy prospect for future sales generated by a planned expansion in production capacity. On closer examination, however, it might transpire that the engineering problems in interfacing the old plant with the new one make the total project uneconomical or an internal policy of paying shareholders bigger dividends and ploughing back less money into expansion might block the project. ④

[12] Project identification is particularly difficult when long lead times are involved, and the factors affecting these decisions vary at an uncomfortable frequency. Much has been written about the dilemma facing the CEGB in the mid-'seventies when their planned expansion predicted in the'sixties did not materialise. The result was an embarrassing number of idle power stations built on decisions made in the previous decade. ⑤

Preparation of scope

[13] Scope, or the extent of the project, was mentioned briefly earlier. This stage will include aspects such as the actual work performed, the programme, the availability of materials, site requirements, and the use of standards.

[14] When the project has been identified, design work must commence to define the precise nature of the project. The Project Manager must decide on either in-house design or a total design and construct package. Usually, if the project is unique, the former is preferable. In instances when the organisation does not have this capability then consultants may be used.

[15] At this stage, the manager is stretched to the utmost, for not only should his technical competence be used, but he must also co-ordinate all design information to ensure that the proposals are held within the various economic and safety constraints that operate. A consultant's design for building finishes on an industrial complex might involve the construction of difficult and uneconomic corners, slopes or curves. Although these proposals enhance the aesthetic appearance of the building, their effect on final costs may be significant enough to necessitate a rethink of the whole scheme.

[16] A programme with a firm completion date must be drawn up. If late completion entails loss of revenue, then this must be evaluated on a time and cost basis. If no income is involved,

as in, say, the construction of a road, then the 'opportunity cost' of this delay should be quantified. Likewise, the advantages of bringing the completion date forward should be known so that possible incentives may be built into the contract.

New Words and Expressions

identification * [ai͵dentifi'keiʃən]	n.	确认；识别
strive [straiv]	v.	努力，力求；斗争
whilst [wailst]	conj.	而；当……的时候
bias * ['baiəs]	v.	使倾向一方；使有偏见
scrutinise ['skru:tinaiz]	v.	仔细检查；详审
interrelated [͵intəri'leitid]	a.	相互关联的；相关的
accelerate [æk'seləreit]	v.	加速；催速
acceleration * [æk͵selə'reiʃən]	n.	加速；促进
quantify * ['kwɔntifai]	v.	确定……的量；用数量表示
assessment [ə'sesmənt]	n.	估计；评价
tender ['tendə]	n.; v.	投标；提出
incentive * [in'sentiv]	n.	鼓励；刺激
penalty * ['penlti]	n.	处罚，惩罚；罚款
lead up to		导致；把……一直带到
repercussion [͵ri:pə'kʌʃən]	n.	影响；反应；相互作用
marketing ['mɑ:kitiŋ]	n.	交易；在市场上买卖
rosy ['rəuzi]	a.	乐观的，光明的；玫瑰色的
transpire [træns'paiə]	v.	为人所知，泄漏；发散，排出
interface ['intəfeis]	v.	连结
	n.	分界面，相交处
uneconomical ['ʌn͵i:kə'nɔmikəl]	a.	不经济的，浪费的
shareholder ['ʃɛə͵həuldə]	n.	股东；股票持有人
dividend ['dividend]	n.	红利，股息；被除数
lead [li:d]	a.	领头的，领先的；最重要的
dilemma [di'lemə]	n.	困境；左右为难的状况
materialise [mə'tiəriəlaiz]	v.	成为事实，实现；物质化
in-house ['inhaus]	a.	机构（组织）内部的；非外部的
finish ['finiʃ]	n.	［建］装饰；完美；结束
complex ['kɔmpleks]	n.	综合企业；复杂，合成物
enhance * [in'hɑ:ns]	v.	增强；提高
rethink [ri:'θiŋk]	n.	重新考虑
entail * [in'teil]	v.	引起；使需要；使承担

Notes

① "others" 与 "towards" 之间省掉了谓语 "are biased"。
② "it" 为形式主语，真正的主语为后面 "to" 引出的不定式短语。
③ 为避免重复，"an assessment" 与 "made" 之间省掉了 "must be"。"these costs will have …" 为定语从句，修饰 "impact"。
④ 该句是由 "or" 连接的两个并列分句组成的；第一个分句中的 "it" 为形式主语，真正的主语为 "that" 引出的名词性从句，该分句的谓语是 "might transpire"；第二个分句的谓语是 "might block"。
⑤ 句中 "built" 和 "made" 都是过去分词，修饰各自前面的名词。

Exercises

Reading Comprehension

Ⅰ. Choose the best answer.

1. The author states that many clients fail to see
    A. a contract is supposed to protect both the client and the contractor.
    B. some contracts are favourable to the contractor while others benefit the client.
    C. there exists great difference in the objectives of the client and the contractor.
    D. a contract is enforceable by law.
2. Which of the following statements can be inferred from the passage?
    A. In a contract, the contractor is more likely to bear risks.
    B. Any variation of the project will entail more labour.
    C. In order to meet the completion date, the employer must decrease the project scope.
    D. One must be cautious in changing the design after placing the contract.
3. Which of the following is NOT suggested as a reason for difficulty of project identification?
    A. It is hard to predict the future.
    B. Factors affecting project identification vary a lot.
    C. The organization's overall corporate plan must be taken into consideration.
    D. Project identification comes first in the pre-contract stages.
4. Which of the following can NOT be inferred about the "power stations"?
    A. They were not put into good use.
    B. People felt uncomfortable at the sight of them.
    C. There were quite a few of them.
    D. They were built in the sixties.

5. To the project manager, the decisive element in scope preparation seems to be
   A. the consultant's proposals.
   B. final costs.
   C. aesthetic aspects.
   D. in-house design.

II. Match Column A with Column B according to the text.

A	B
1. project scope	a. design made within an organization or its facilities
2. finish	b. call for an offer of a bid for a contract
3. in-house design	c. a formal agreement between two or more people to do something
4. contract	d. a whole made up of a large number of closely related parts
5. invite tenders	e. the extent or area a project covers
	f. a punishment for breaking a legal agreement
	g. something that completes or perfects, as the fine or decorative work required for a building

Vocabulary

I. Fill in the blanks with the expressions given below. Change the form if necessary.

> market, phase, penalty, tender, plough back

1. Fierce arguments may arise in the administration _____ of a contract.
2. Common Market countries, one of the economic giants of the world, are _____ much of their yearly outputs into new construction and equipment.
3. Every contractor who has received the _____ must be informed of such aspects as access to a construction site, ground conditions and any work restrictions.
4. Most target cost contracts contain a bonus or _____ clause and even a loss-sharing scheme, which are useful when a particularly difficult project is envisaged.
5. When a company decides it needs long-term funds by _____ stocks and bonds, it must find people to buy them.

II. Use words from the text to complete the following sentences. Change the form if necessary.

1. Government budgets deal not only with expenditures, but also with _____, which are raised through taxation.
2. If stock insurance companies make a profit as a result of low losses, at the end of a year, company profits will be paid to stockholders in the form of _____.

3. The _____ built into the contract can help to keep down cost, improve technical performance and meet completion dates.
4. The contractor still makes allowances for all possible weather, environmental, or site conditions that may _____ the successful completion of the project.
5. Since final costs are based on plans and drawings, it is imperative that there are no changes or variations after the contract is _____.

Reading Material A

Selection of Contract Strategy

The main objective in this activity is selecting a contract that will work to the employer's advantage and so provide successful completion at minimum cost. One must look closely at the expected relationship between client and contractor, of which there are several variants. At one end of the spectrum there exists the 'cost plus' contract and at the other the 'lump sum'.

It is worth looking at the various popular types of contract that are currently in use. These will hopefully, give assistance in the selection of a contract strategy.

Cost plus contracts

The greatest client risk is probably borne by this type of contract. The contractor receives all costs incurred in the execution of the project, plus a percentage for profit or overhead charges. Costs, overheads, and percentage mark-ups are defined before placing the contract. This system is used when the scope of work is ill-defined and difficult to predict.

Target cost contracts

Most target cost contracts contain a bonus or penalty clause and even sometimes a loss-sharing scheme. They are useful when dealing with one-off jobs, or when a particularly difficult project is envisaged. The contract seeks to set up competition between prime costs and a hypothetical 'standard cost'.

Incentives can be provided under this type of contract. Built-in incentives can help to keep down cost, improve technical performance and meet completion dates. This is achieved by having a target cost, a 'target fee', and a 'sharing formula'. The target fee is payable as a profit if the out-turn prices are that of the target cost and a sharing formula will determine how excess cost or savings are shared between client and contractor.[1]

Measure and value contracts

These are contracts based on a quoted schedule of rates in an approximate Bill of Quantities. Although these are really fixed-rate contracts, some people refer to them as lump sum contracts. The advantage with this system for the client is that the risk lies with the contractor and there exists a definite structure for financially controlling the project. As these quantities and rates are based on plans and drawings, it is imperative that there are no changes or variations after placing the contract.

Lump sum contracts

These are based on drawings or specifications and are truly lump sum contracts. The disadvantage here is that any small change in design or other similar variation cannot be priced with the accuracy afforded by a fixed Bill of Quantities. Instead, the employer has to negotiate a new lump sum rate in view of the variations. This is to be recommended only for routine jobs which have been tried and tested.

Package deal contracts

In this arrangement both design and construction are handled by the same contractor. It eliminates one source of claim, viz., those of drawing or design error.[2] However, it should be remembered that the contractor is in the business to make a profit and to cover himself.[3] In the end, design work done in this way is likely to be more expensive than that done by in-house methods.

We have now discussed the various types of contracts. The following factors should be given consideration before any particular type is adopted:

a) the nature of work to be performed and the method of construction,

b) the depth of necessary information available at the time of appointing the contractor,

c) the location of the project,

d) timing and rate of working,

e) the macro-economic position in relation to the upward or downward movement of labour and material rates,

f) the availability of labour, materials and contractors,

g) degree of financial control required.

Notes

①如果实际价格与标定费用一致，那么标定费用就以利润形式支付，而其分成方案将会决定怎样将超额费用或剩余款项分摊给业主和承包人。

②这样就消除了一个要求索赔的渠道，即由于绘图或设计错误导致的索赔要求。

③承包商之所以承接这个项目，就是为了赚取利润，使自己不亏本，这一点应该牢记在心。

Reading Material B

Preparation of Tender Documents

The successful ingredients of good tender documents are:
1. Reduce complexity to a minimum.
2. Eliminate all ambiguity.
3. Check all drawings thoroughly, and ensure that all standards referred to are issued.
4. Ensure all documents agree with each other
5. Clearly specify programme and the precise extent or definition of completion.

It is in the interest of the client to achieve the closest tendering possible thus, every contractor receiving the tender must be given parity of information. Aspects such as access to a construction site, ground conditions, overall geology, and any working restrictions must be clearly specified. When the contractors are in receipt of the tenders, this information should be backed up by pre-tender meetings. Here the tenderer is invited to ask the prospective client any questions pertaining to the bid. This meeting, which may involve a visit to site, if any, should take place in the presence of all the other bidders and should be backed up by accurate minutes.①

Handling a tender enquiry in this way should eliminate much of the fierce arguments that may arise in the administration phase of a contract. The most usual claim is that the original price build-ups did not allow for conditions actually encountered by the contractor. At the same time, there is no longer the danger of eliminating the diligent contractor who makes overgenerous allowances for all ambiguities.②

A typical clause which estimators detest may read: "The contractor shall make allowances for all possible weather, environmental, or site conditions that may defer the successful completion".

A very common claim for extra cost is that arising out of errors in the original tender drawings.③ Cases where dimensions do not add up, where modifications are inconsistent, or where material numbers do not match are the most frequent offenders.④ Care must be taken to ensure that such errors do not exist.

It is also necessary to include a programme, the presentation of which may vary from a single bar, indicating 'start' and 'finish', to a detailed activity network.⑤ The latter is sometimes necessary when the project involves imposed time constraints on certain sections of the work.⑥ During the building of a process plant, for a instance, at some stage an activity may involve the installation of a compressor. The unit comes as a package from a foreign manufacturer, and will not be due until the end of the project. This activity must, therefore, be placed at a suitable point at the end of the programme.

List of tender documents

The following documents must accompany any invitation to tender:

1. A letter of invitation.

2. The conditions of tender. The contractor must be assured that is quote will be treated fairly. Estimating is a time-consuming exercise, so any abortive work is unwelcome. The final date for receipt of tenders should be clearly stated, and the arrangements for any pre-tender meetings included.⑦

3. The general conditions of contract. Usually it will suffice to refer to these if a well-known contract code is used.

4. Special conditions of contract. Include any conditions in addition to those mentioned above in (3). However, it should be remembered that the standard conditions have been evolved by experts after much consideration and discussion. Any changes or additions to these conditions could present more problems than are bargained for.⑧

5. Specifications. These should include all specifications (technical and non-technical) needed to carry out the project successfully. Again, if a well-known specification or standard, such as the British Standards, is used, then mere reference to it is adequate.

6. The plans, drawings, and other diagrammatic representations.

7. The Bill of Quantities (BOQ). This is a schedule of work elements or activities, required to execute the contract. Each of these items is priced by the contractor, and is peculiar to measurable contracts.

Notes

①这种会议可能会包括现场参观（如果有现场的话），它应该在所有其他投标人在场的情况下进行，并且要有准确的会议记录。
②同时，再也不用担心会有那种用心良苦，对所有有空子可钻的地方都作出过分慷慨承诺的承包商了。
③要求增加额外开支十之八九是由于投标图纸出现错误而产生。
④尺寸不合理，前后修改不一致，或材料数量有出入，这些都常常是最叫人伤脑筋的事情。
⑤同时有必要制定一项方案，它包括小至一横道表示起始和结束，大至一个详细的活动网络系统。
⑥如果对项目的某些阶段有时间限制，那么后者是必不可少的。
⑦接受投标的截止日期应明确写出，而且对任何投标前的碰头会的安排也应包括在内。
⑧对这些条件的任何修改或增补都可能导致比预想的要多的问题。

UNIT SIXTEEN

Text　　　Contractor/Sub-contractor Relationships（Ⅰ）

INTRODUCTION

[1]　The relationship between main contractor and sub-contractor is a human one and the aim of this paper is to provide an appreciation of the problems they both experience and by so doing attempt to resolve them to the benefit of all members of the building team.

TYPES OF MAIN CONTRACTOR

[2]　　Contractors may be classified into three groups:
　　　——the national contractor;
　　　——the town or city contractor;
　　　——the small builder.

[3]　This classification does not cover all builders but it is convenient for the purposes of this paper.

The national contractor

[4]　　The national contractor is usually a public limited liability company responsible to its shareholders and managed through its directors who may be professionally or technically qualified.① Its attitude to sub-contractors, therefore, may be more remote than smaller contractors.②

[5]　　Operations will be on a national basis and, consequently, there will be a closer relationship with the larger, nationally based sub-contractors. Once having established a good relationship with a sub-contractor there will be a strong disincentive to change.

[6]　　The national contractor probably experiences less competition than other contractors due to the size of work he can undertake. Favourable terms can, therefore, be negotiated with specialists who complement this mode of operation.

The town or city contractor

[7]　The area of operations of this type of company is more circumscribed and greater use is, therefore, made of local sub-contractors. The firm is often a family concern and generally has

138

a strong regard for the quality of its product, although profit is still the aim. Each building tends to be a monument to the company as all concerned will enjoy the same environment as the buildings they construct.③ The directors or proprietors will have a direct interest in the operation of the firm since they will be involved with estimating, contract management, surveying or site management.

The small builder

[8]　The small builder tends to operate within a restricted geographical area. The principal will often work on the site and generally has more practical experience than technical knowledge. The small builder is usually a good tradesman and produces a satisfactory job for his client. He will tend to deal with the small sub-contractor who will operate on the same contractual basis.

TYPES OF SUB-CONTRACTOR

[9]　A breakdown of the main types of sub-contractor and their principal areas of operation is given at the appendix. They are the:

——specialist sub-contractor;

——trade sub-contractor;

——labour only sub-contractor.

Specialist sub-contractor

[10]　The specialist sub-contractor provides a design and fix service and is usually nominated. He quotes for work in limited competition and is efficient due to the repetitive nature of the work. Such sub-contractors find it essential to have a selling organisation with technical representatives calling on architects and contractors.④

[11]　To enable the architect to make a selection from a number of specialist sub-contractors, the sub-contractor may be asked to prepare a design, relating to the project, to accompany his quotation.⑤ This represents an additional expense which will need to be reflected in the firm's overheads.

Trade sub-contractor

[12]　The trade sub-contractor is selected invariably by the main contractor but it is often a contractual condition that the architect has to approve the selection. He has a close and continuing contact with the builder. He carries out all the traditional trades but rarely needs selling expertise, as his past performance is his selling potential. Generally, no design service is of-

fered, just labour, materials and supervision. His overheads should, therefore, be less than the specialist sub-contractor.

Labour only sub-contractor

[13] Recent years have seen a dramatic change from the direct employment of operatives to the employment of labour only sub-contractors. On some contracts, particularly repetitive units such as housing, it is not unusual for the whole of the contract to be carried out with sub-contracted labour.

[14] Arising from the increase in the employment of labour only sub-contractors, legislation was introduced to control the tax payments from this type of sub-contractor, known as the 714 Certificate.⑥ The main contractor must satisfy himself that the sub-contractor is in possession of a valid certificate issued by the Inland Revenue. Failing which he must deduct 30% of the value of work carried out from the sub-contractor's payment.⑦

[15] Many of these sub-contractors, therefore, are now correctly constituted firms giving a valuable service to the industry and are a competitive (due to low overheads) alternative to direct labour.

New Words and Expressions

liability * [ˌlaiə'biliti]	n.	责任；债务
disincentive [ˌdisin'sentiv]	n.	障碍；抑制
negotiate [ni'gəuʃieit]	v.	议定，议妥；谈判
complement * ['kɔmpliment]	v.	补足，补充
circumscribe ['səːkəmskraib]	v.	限制；约束
have a strong regard for		非常注重；特别关心
proprietor [prə'praiətə]	n.	所有人，业主
tradesman ['treidzmən]	n.	手艺人；商人；店主
contractual [kən'træktjuəl]	a.	契约的；契约性的
appendix * [ə'pendiks]	n.	附录；附属物
repetitive * [ri'petitiv]	a.	重复的；反复的
quotation [kwəu'teiʃən]	n.	报价单；引用，引文
invariably * [in'vɛəriəbli]	ad.	总是；不变地
operative ['ɔpərətiv]	n.	技工
	a.	操作的，有效的
legislation [ˌledʒis'leiʃən]	n.	法规；立法
satisfy ['sætisfai]	v.	说服，使相信，向……证实；使……满足
deduct [di'dʌkt]	v.	扣除，减去；演绎

Notes

① 句中"responsible to its shareholders"与过去分词短语"managed..."都修饰前面的名词"company"。

② 为避免重复,句中的"smaller contractors"之后省去了"to sub-contractors"。

③ 句中有两个"as"。第一个"as"引出一个表原因的从句,第二个"as"是词组"the same ... as"中的一部分;"they construct"为定语从句,修饰"buildings"。

④ 句中"it"作"find"的形式宾语,真正宾语为不定式短语"to have...";"with..."为介词短语,修饰其前面的"organisation",其中"technical architects"是介词"with"的宾语,"calling..."则为宾语补足语。

⑤ 句中"relating to the project"为分词短语,作定语,修饰名词"design";"to accompany his quotation"为不定式短语,在句中作目的状语。

⑥ "known..."为过去分词短语,在句中作定语,修饰"legislation"。

⑦ 句中"failing which"意即"unable to satisfy himself that the sub-contractor is in possession of a valid certificate...";"he"指前句中的"the main contractor"。

Exercises

Reading Comprehension

I. Choose the best answer.

1. According to the author, which of the following puts national contractors in an advantageous position?

   A. They are granted the most favourable terms.

   B. They are endowed with specialists who can improve their design.

   C. Their directors are professionally qualified.

   D. They have more capacity for fulfilling challenging tasks.

2. Why do town contractors attach great importance to the quality of their products?

   A. They believe the product bespeaks the producer.

   B. Their families are deeply concerned for their products.

   C. They seldom undertake big enterprises.

   D. The contractors themselves will live in the buildings they construct.

3. The town or city contractor is more likely to deal with

   A. small sub-contractors.

   B. local sub-contractors.

   C. nationally based sub-contractors.

   D. specialist sub-contractors.

4. It can be inferred from the passage that the "certificate" is related with
   A. the firm's overheads.
   B. tax payments.
   C. the quotation of the work.
   D. the labour only sub-contractor's additional expenses.
5. Which of the following accounts for the popularity of the employment of labour only sub-contractors?
   A. They require low overheads.
   B. They have established their own companies.
   C. They are protected by law.
   D. They possess valid certificates.

Ⅱ. Say whether the following statements are True (T) or False (F) according to the text.
(　　) 1. The small builder has the most restricted area of operation.
(　　) 2. The specialist sub-contractor is supposed to call on architects and contractors.
(　　) 3. The trade sub-contractor advises the architect of the costs associated with the work.
(　　) 4. Labour only sub-contractors are so competitive that they are likely to take the place of operatives.
(　　) 5. Trade sub-contractor needs less overheads than the specialist subcontractor since he does not have to provide labour, materials and supervision.

Vocabulary

Ⅰ. Fill in the blanks with the expressions given below. Change the form if necessary.

satisfy, building team, condition, operative, certificate

1. Should the specialist work fall behind the programme, the contractor could point out to the sub-contractor that there are not sufficient _____ on site.
2. The quantity surveyor can provide information which will enable the contractor's surveyor to include the true cost in interim _____ and to prepare accurate monthly cost comparisons.
3. The contractor is required to comply with the _____ of the contract.
4. It is advisable for all members of the _____ to be present at regular site progress meeting, viz., architect, quantity surveyor, consultant, contractor's agent, plus sub-contractors and their representatives.
5. Only if the bank is _____ that the customer's credit standing is reasonable, will it grant him the loan.

Ⅱ. Complete the following sentences with words from the text, making use of the given paragraph reference number.
1. Since their absence at a critical time can ruin the programme, all the participants must be made aware of their damages _____ due to the delay. (Para. 4)

2. It is advisable for the main contractor to state the access and availability of storage space and other facilities so that the sub-contractor can take this into consideration when preparing his _____. (Para. 11)
3. Late _____ is the major cause of bad feeling, therefore, it is in the contractor's own interests to pay promptly. (Para. 14)
4. Income taxes are based on net income, i.e. what remains after certain items are _____ from gross income. (Para. 14)
5. We can buy insurance from a _____ of the insurance company who is known as an insurance agent. (Para. 10)

Reading Material A

Contractor/Sub-contractor Relationships (II)

Contractual Responsibilities

The members of the project team and their prime functions are as follows:

The architect

The architect produces the design and attempts to combine aesthetics with functional integrity. Ideally, he must be in a position to appoint all the nominated sub-contractors prior to awarding the main contract and to approve all specialist's submitted drawings in sufficient time to allow the work to be carried out within the programme period.①

The quantity surveyor

The quantity surveyor advises the architect of the costs associated with the design, prepares bills of quantities to allow tenders to be submitted, and monitors and controls the costs during construction. When variations occur during a contract it is generally desirable for all parties to be aware of their cost implications as soon as possible. The quantity surveyor can perform a valuable service in this respect since the information he provides will:
——enable the contractor's surveyor to include the true cost in interim certificates and to prepare accurate monthly cost comparisons;
——allow the quantity surveyor to keep the architect and client informed concerning actual cost;
——ensure that the contractor and sub-contractor receive payment for work carried out in the month's valuation in which it occurred.

The consultant

Consultants advise the architect on the specialist functions of the building such as foundations, load bearing structures and all works of a specialised nature.

The main contractor

The main contractor is required to comply with the conditions of contract and will need to co-ordinate the work of all sub-contractors to ensure the smooth progress of the contract. He is responsible for arranging regular site progress meetings to:
—— review work completed;
—— discuss work under construction;
—— consider matters of immediate importance;
—— resolve current problems;
—— advise on action taken;
—— discuss items likely to cause delay.

It is advisable for all members of the building team to be present at these meetings, viz. architect, quantity surveyor, consultant, contractor's agent, plus representatives of sub-contractors whose work will be commencing during the next month and sub-contractors whose work is in progress on the contract. [2]

The sub-contractor

The sub-contractor is required to meet the conditions of sub-contract but in addition he may have design responsibilities.

He co-operates with the main contractor by attending site meetings to see how his work integrates with that of other sub-contractors and that of the main contractor. [3]

Similarity of Objectives

Each team member is dependent upon the correct functioning of the others. For example, the architect and quantity surveyor are responsible to their client; the contractor and sub-contractor have to satisfy the architect's requirement. If the contract is not carried out successfully then the architect loses prestige and further commissions and the contractor and sub-contractor are not invited to tender for further projects.

Therefore, a successful contract should be the objective of all. One of the architect's major responsibilities is to see that the contractor has sufficient information to enable him to carry out the contract within the programmed time. Lack of information will not only raise claims from subcontractors to contractor and then to architect and eventually to client but it will have an extremely detrimental effect on the harmony and relationship between all parties.④ Therefore, it cannot be stressed too much that it is in every team member's interest to try to look ahead and advise in plenty of time any item that it is likely to cause a delay, so that adequate steps can be taken to mitigate the delay, from which no one really benefits.⑤

Notes

①理想的作法是，在交付总合同之前，建筑师应该有权任命所有被提名的分包商，并能及时批准专家呈上来的所有设计方案，以使工程能在计划期内进行。

②建筑队的所有成员最好都能出席这些会议。这些成员包括建筑师、工料测量师、顾问、承包商代理，外加分包商代理人和分包商，分包商代理将在后一个月开始工作，而分包商则在合同签订之时就投入工作了。

③分包商出席现场会议以配合总承包商的工作，并以此了解自己的工作是怎样同其它分包商及总承包商的工作合为一体的。

④若缺少信息，分包商就会首先向承包商、继而向建筑师、最终向业主提出要求，不仅如此，信息不通还会给所有当事人之间的协调和关系带来极坏的影响。

⑤向前看，并且及时告知各方有可能导致延误的工程项目，以便采取适当的措施来使那种谁也不能真正获利的拖延得以缓解，这样做符合建筑队所有成员的利益，所以对此再怎样强调都不为过分。

Reading Material B

Contractor/Sub-contractor Relationships（Ⅲ）

Problem Areas

Pre-contract

It is important that nominated sub-contractors are selected and that their contract periods are known to the main contractor at the pre-contract stage. For the architect to have a successful contract it is a prime pre-requisite for him to see that this information is available for the successful contractor so that he may incorporate the sub-contractors' respective time periods into the contract draft programme of work.

During the contract

As the success of any contract will depend on the establishment of a workable understanding by all involved, it is essential that pre-consultation is carried out between main contractor and sub-contractor when the final programme of work is being prepared. If all the participants are aware of the importance of their roles and how their non-appearance at a critical time can ruin the programme, they are more likely to co-operate. If all other means fail, then as a last resort they must be made aware of their damages liability due to their delay.

Shared use of plant

When a main contractor seeks quotations from sub-trades, it is always advisable for him to state the access and availability of storage space so that the sub-contractor can take this into consideration when preparing his quotation. He should also give details of the plant that may be available for use, such as scaffolding, canteen facilities, and special plant such as tower cranes. Regarding the latter it may be the policy of the main contractor to offer the tower crane as a facility and ask the sub-contractor to allow for this within his quotation.① Alternatively, he may charge for use of the tower crane per hour in which case he would need to state this in his quotation enquiry.② It is usual for the conditions of contract to state that a specialist subcontractor will be provided with sand and cement and scaffolding (either as erected or special). However, in some cases, a number of sub-contractors will need to draw on basic materials.

In this situation it is advisable for a simple form to be employed which states the amount of material used. The appropriate charge can then be made at the interim valuation stage.

Progress

The specialist should know the number of operatives to send to the site to carry out the work within the programme period. Should the specialist work fall behind the programme, the contractor could then point out to the sub-contractor that there are not sufficient operatives on site.

Programmes of work should be drawn up carefully. The contractor may produce initially a simple bar chart from which he will advise the sub-contractors of the approximate dates the site will be available.③ As work progresses, the sub-contractors must be advised of delays and programme revisions made to enable them to adjust their own labour programme.④

Appointment of nominated sub-contractors

When the architect has selected his sub-contractors the main contractor has the right to object to any nomination before entering into the sub-contract.

The main grounds for objection lie in unsatisfactory past performance in relation to workmanship or progress. If, however, an objection is made and over-ruled the contract would not commence on a favourable basis. It is suggested, therefore, that if such a situation arises a meeting should be arranged between the architect, main contractor and sub-contractor to ensure that the position is made clear. ⑤

Payment

The main contractor is most concerned to receive payment within the prescribed period. It is not unusual, on the other hand, not to recognise a similar requirement on the part of his sub-contractor. Late payment is perhaps the major cause of bad feeling —— it is in the contractor's own interests to pay promptly.

Notes

①说起后者,总承包商的政策当是提供塔式起重机这种设备,然后让分包商将此算进报价单里。
②或者,他也可以论小时收取起重机使用费。在这种情况下,他得在询价书中将此明确写出。
③承包商可以首先拿出一个简单的横道图,以此他会告知各分包商工地可交付使用的大致日期。
④随着工程的进展,必须告诉分包商有关工程的延误及方案的修改情况,以使分包商能调整自己的施工计划。
⑤因此建议如果发生此类情况,应当安排一次建筑师、总承包商和分包商的碰头会,以确保大家弄清形势。

Appendix I Vocabulary

accelerate	v. 加速；催速	15
acceleration*	n. 加速；促进	15
accountant	n. 会计员,会计师	08
accountant	n. 会计	04
accounting	n. 会计学；会计	11
accumulation	n. 积累；积聚物	14
acqusition*	n. 取得,获得,获得物	08
adhere to	固守,忠于,坚持	11
administer	vt. 管理,支配；执行,实施	11
adventurously	a. 带有冒险性地；带有危险性地	02
adviser	n. 顾问	04
aesthetic	a. 美学的；美的,艺术的	13
agenda	n. 议事日程；记事本	09
aggregate*	a. 合计的,聚集的	09
	v. 聚集,集合	09
	n. 集合,聚合	09
allocate	v. 把(物质,资金等)划归,分配	11
ambitious	a. 炫耀的；有雄心的	02
amenity	n. 令人愉快的东西	02
amortize	v. 分期偿还；转让	14
anticipate	v. 提前使用,预算	04
appendix*	n. 附录；附属物	16
appreciation	n. 涨价,增值；估计	14
arbitration	n. 仲裁,调解	07
architect*	n. 建筑师	05
arduousness	n. 艰巨,艰苦	02
assessment	n. 估计；评价	15
asset	n. [复]资产,财产	01
assurance	n. 保证；保险	07
at stake	利害(生死)悠关,在危险中	08
at variance	(事物间)不符；(人和人)有分歧；不和	09
attributable*	a. 可归因于…的,由…引起的	07
authorize,-ise	vt. 批准,允许,认可；授权,委任	12
availability	n. 可得性,可得到的东西	02
bank credit	银行信贷	09
banker	n. 银行家	04
be adequate to do …	适于做…,足以做…	03
bias*	v. 使倾向一方；使有偏见	15
bid*	v.;n. 投标,出价	04
bid*	v. 投标；出价	05
bidder	n. 投标人；出价人	05
bonding company	担保公司	04
boom*	n. (市面的)忽然兴旺；繁荣；(形势的)突然好转	06
boost	v. 提高	01
borrower	n. 借用者,借贷者	04
breach	n. 违反,不履行	12
brickwork	n. 砌砖；砖房,砖瓦工	13
budget*	n. 预算	07
	v. 编预算	07
bulky*	a. 庞大的,笨大的	03
capricious	a. 反复无常的,无定见的	01
caption	n. (文件,文章等)标题,(图片等)解说词	04
circumscribe	v. 限制；约束	16
cite*	v. 引用,引证；传讯	10
clearance*	n. 净空,间隙,余隙	09
client	n. 委托人；业主	03
closure*	n. 截止；关闭	05
cognizant	a. 认识的,知晓的	11

148

collectibility	n.	收集,征收,可收集性	04
collection	n.	收款,收帐,收入款项	04
comform *	v.	使符合,使一致;依照	07
commence *	v.	开始	10
comparable *	a.	可比较的,类似的	1
compensate for *		补偿	13
compensation *	n.	赔偿;补偿(金)	07
competence	n.	能力,胜任,资格	11
competitive *	a.	竞争的;竞赛的	06
complement *	v.	补足,补充	16
completion *	n.	完成,结束	05
complex	n.	综合企业;复杂,合成物	15
complexity	n.	复杂(性),复杂的事物	03
comply	vi.	(与 with 连用)遵守;照做	05
comply with	v.	照做,遵守	12
component	n.	构件,组成部分	02
concurrent	a.	同时发生的,并存的	12
conical	a.	圆锥形的	02
consequent	a.	随之发生的;因…而起的	06
consequential	a.	作为结果的;重大的	07
consolation	n.	安慰(物);抚恤(金)	07
constraint *	n.	约束,强制(力)	08
consultant *	n.	顾问;咨询者	07
consultation	n.	商议;参考	05
consumer *	n.	消费者,用户	07
contemplate	v.	打算;考虑	05
contractor *	n.	承包商;包工头	03
contractual	a.	契约的;契约性的	16
corporate *	a.	社团的,法人的,共同的	11
cost-plus fee		成本加费用酬金	04
craftsman	n.	手艺人,工匠	03
creditor	n.	债权人;贷方,贷项	11
criterion *	n. pl.-ria	(批评,判断的)标准,准则	08
cross-fertilise	v.	(植)使异花受精;(喻)使相互补充而得益	02
custodianship	n.	保管人的责任,保管人的资格	11
customarily	ad.	通常;习惯上	05
cutback	n.	削减;中止	06
cyclical *	a.	周期的,循环的,轮转的	09
deduct	v.	扣除,减去;演绎	16
defective	a.	有缺陷(缺点)的,有瑕疵的	08
deferment	n.	迟延;延期	14
deficient	a.	不足的;缺乏的	13
deficit	n.	赤字,亏空	01
deliberately	ad.	故意地,畜意地	11
demolition	n.	拆毁,破坏	09
depreciation	n.	折旧;跌价	09
designate *	vt.	指定,选派	05
desirability	n.	可取之处;好处,优点	13
differentiation	n.	分化,变异;区别	10
dilemma	n.	困境;左右为难的状况	15
diminution	n.	减少;减缩,缩小	06
disaggregation	n.	解集作用,聚集体分开成为它的构成部分	09
disastrous	a.	造成惨重损失的,灾难性的	04
discernible	a.	看得清的;辨别得出的	02
disharmony	n.	不协调;不调和	06
disincentive	n.	障碍;抑制	16
disrupt	v.	破坏,瓦解	01
disruption *	n.	分裂;瓦解;破裂	06
dividend	n.	红利,股息;被除数	15
document	v.	为…提出文件(或证明书),用文件说明	12
down payment		定金	14
downturn	n.	下降趋势;下转	06
drainage	n.	排水(设备)下水道	13

149

effctiveness *	n. 效率；有效性	06	
elements	n. （复）风雨，自然力	02	
elimination	n. 除去，消灭	08	
elongate *	v. （使）延长；拉长	13	
endeavo(u)r	n. 努力，尽力	12	
	v. 努力，尽力，力图	12	
enforceable	a. 可强制服从的；可实施的	07	
enhance *	v. 增强；提高	15	
entail *	v. 引起；使需要；使承担	15	
enterprise *	n. 企（事）业单位；兴办（企业）	06	
entity	n. 实体，统一体	11	
entrepreneurial	a. 企业家的，关于企业家的	10	
entrust(to)	v. 托管，委托	11	
envisage	vt. 展望，设想	09	
equilibrium *	n. 平衡；均势；不偏不倚	14	
equity	n. （押款金额以外的）财产价值；股票；公平，公道	14	
erection	n. 建造；建立；安装	03	
essence	n. 本质，实质，精华	07	
exacerbate	vt. 使（病，痛等）加重	10	
expenditure *	n. （金钱，时间等的）支出，花费；费用	06	
expenditure *	n. 支出，支出额，消费额	04	
explicit *	a. 显然可见的；明晰的	14	
extract	v. 选取；提取	03	
facet	n. （题目，思想等）某一方面	03	
facilitate	v. 使容易；促进	03	
feasibility *	n. 可行性，可能性	14	
finish	n. 【建】装饰；完美；结束	15	
fiscal	a. 国库的；（美）财政的，公款的	09	
flexibility *	n. 柔(韧)性，灵活性	03	
fluctuation	n. 起伏，涨落，波动	09	
forego	v. 放弃；发生在……之前	14	
formulate *	v. 对…作简洁陈述，有系统地表达；用公式表示	08	
forward	vt. 转送；发送	05	
free enterprise	（企业的）自由经营	11	
fruition	n. 实现；完成	02	
gamble	n. 投机，冒险；赌博	14	
gross domestic product	国民生产总值；国内总产值	09	
hardheaded	a. 冷静的，精明而讲实际的	04	
have a strong regard for	非常注重；特别关心	16	
herein *	ad. 在此处，此中	05	
highlight	v. 集中注意力于，着重	10	
homeowner	n. 房主	01	
homeownership	n. 房主地位	01	
housholder	n. 占有房子的人；住户；户主	02	
hub	n. 中心，中枢	08	
identification *	n. 确认；识别	15	
implement *	vt. 实现 实施	10	
implementation	n. 贯彻，实现	09	
imprecise	a. 不精确的，不明确的	07	
in essence	本质上，大体上	07	
in progress	ad. 在进行中，在发展中	12	
in-house	a. 机构（组织）内部的；非外部的	15	
inadequate *	a. 不充足的；不适当的	07	
incentive *	n. 鼓励；刺激	15	
incorporate *	v. 使具体化，体现；合并；纳入，结合	02	
indebted	a. 负债的	01	
indicative *	a. 指示的，预示的	04	
indivisibility	n. 不可分性	10	
induce *	vt. 引起，导致；引诱，劝使	10	
indulge (in)	v. 沉迷，沉溺	04	
inefficiency	n. 无效；有效	16	
inflation	n. 通货膨胀，物价飞涨	01	
inflationary	a. 膨胀的；通货膨胀的	10	

词条	词性	释义	页码
inseparable	a.	不可分离的	14
insider	n.	内部人,局内人,知情人	11
institutional	a.	惯例的;制度上的;公共机构的	03
intact *	a.	未受损的;完整无损的	06
interact *	v.	相互作用,相互影响	03
interdependent	a.	互相依赖的,互相依存的	09
interface	v.	连结	
	n.	分界面,相交处	15
interrelated	a.	相互关联的;相关的	15
invariably *	ad.	总是;不变地	16
inventory *	v.	为…编制目录,开列存货清单	04
investor	n.	投资者	01
irreducible	a.	不能降低(或削减)的,不能缩小的	10
irritation	n.	不快;激怒	07
joinery	n.	细木工技术(或行业);细木工	10
juggle	v.	玩把戏,耍花招	04
know to one's cost		某人吃亏后才明白	07
lead	a.	领头的,领先的;最重要的	15
lead up to		导致;把……一直带到	15
lease	v.	出租,租用	06
legislation	n.	法规;立法	16
level	v.	使同等;拉平	06
leverage	n.	杠杆作用;影响,力量	14
liability *	n.	责任;债务	16
liquidity	n.	流畅,流动性	06
locality *	n.	位置,地点,所在地	03
log	n.	(工作,航行)记录	05
long-standing	a.	持久不衰的,长期存在的	09
look to sb. for …		指望某人……	02
lump sum work		总额包干工作,金额一次总付的工作	04
lump-sum	a.	一次总付的	05
lure	v.	诱惑;吸引	14
macroeconomics	n.	宏观经济学,大经济学	01
make reference to		提及,涉及;参考,查询	12
make strenuous efforts		尽全力	10
make/use one's best endevors		尽最大努力	12
managerial	a.	管理的;经理的	08
managerial	a.	管理上的,经营上的	10
margin	n.	盈利,毛利;押金,保证金	04
marked *	a.	显著的,清楚的	09
marketing	n.	交易;在市场上买卖	15
materialise	v.	成为事实,实现;物质化	15
maximization	n.	最大限度化	14
maximize	v.	使…增加(扩大)到最大限度;找出…的最高值	08
microeconomic	a.	微观经济(上)的	09
minimal *	a.	最小的;最低的	06
minimize *	v.	使减到最少,按最小限度估计	08
minute	v.	记录,将…制成备忘录	12
	n.	[复]会议记录	12
misinterpretation	n.	曲解;误释	07
misleading	a.	引入歧途的;使人误解的	04
mitigate	v.	缓和;减轻	06
modification *	n.	修改;改进	05
monetary	a.	钱的,货币的,金融的	09
monumental	a.	纪念的;巨大的	02
morale	n.	士气,精神;信心	06
mortgage	n. & v.	抵押	01
mutually	ad.	相互地;彼此地	05
myriad	n.	无数,极大数量	10
necessitate *	v.	使成为必要(需)	03
negotiate	v.	议定,议妥;谈判	16
negotiation	n.	协商;谈判	05
nominate	v.	指定,任命,提名	12
notable *	a.	显著的;值得注意的;著名的	06

151

英文	词性	中文	页码
notification	n.	通知书,通知	12
notify	v.	通知,报告	12
numerical *	a.	数字的,用数字表示的	08
obligation	n.	义务,责任	12
obsolescence	n.	废弃,废退;逐渐过时	10
obsolete *	a.	过时的,陈腐的,已不用的	04
occupancy	n.	(土地,房屋等之)占有,占用	05
offset *	v.	抵销;弥补	13
ominous	a.	不祥的,不吉的;预兆的	06
operative	n.	技工	16
	a.	操作的,有效的	16
option *	n.	选择,取舍;选择权	08
outsider	n.	局外人,外人,外行	11
overhead	n.	企业一般管理费,(商业)间接费用	04
overly	ad.	过度地,过分地	04
overwork	n.	繁重工作;过渡劳累	06
participant *	n.	参与者;参加者	14
partition *	v.	分开,隔开;划分	13
pass on		传给(另外的人),传下去	02
payroll	n.	工资单,工资额	04
penalty *	n.	处罚,惩罚;罚款	15
per se		本身,本来,本质上	09
perimeter	n.	周长,周边	13
periodic	a.	定期的;周期的	05
periodically	ad.	定期的;周期地	05
persuasive	a.	有说服本领的,嘴巧的	06
pertain	v.	适合;关于;属于	03
pertinent *	a.	和…有关的,关于…的,相干的	08
plausible	a.	似乎有理的,似乎可能的	10
plumbing	n.	管子工作,铅管业;(总称)管件	02
police	v.	管治;控制;监视	10
pose *	v.	提出,形成	10
practicable	a.	能实行的,行得通的	13
predictable	a.	可预报的,可预言的	04
premise *	n. pl	房屋(及其附属基地、建筑等);前提;根据	06
prequalification	n.	事先审查	05
presumably *	ad.	大概,可能	11
procurement *	n.	实现,获得;达成	07
productivity	n.	生产率,生产能力	01
profitable *	a.	有益的,有利可图的	04
progress payment		施工分期付款	04
prohibitively *	ad.	…得令人不敢问津	13
pronounced	a.	显著的,明显的	09
pronouncement	n.	见解,表态,声明	11
proposition *	n.	提议;主张	13
proprietor	n.	所有人,业主	16
prospective	a.	有希望的;预期的	05
proviso	n.	限定性条款,附文,(附带)条件	12
put...in		使陷入(某种处境)	12
qualitative *	a.	性质上的,质量上的;定性的	08
quantify *	v.	确定……的量;用数量表示;	15
quantitative *	a.	(数)量的,定量的	08
quotation	n.	报价单,引用,引文	16
radically	a.	根本地,基本地,激进地	02
ready to hand		就在手边的;随手可得的	02
real estate		房地产,不动产	14
realism	n.	(对人对事等)现实主义态度	04
recession	n.	(工商业的)衰退;(价格的)暴跌	06
recognisable	a.	可承认(公认)的;面熟的	06
recompense	n.	报酬,报答;赔偿,补偿	12
rectangular *	a.	长方形的,矩形的	13
redundant *	a.	过多的,过剩的;冗长的	06
rehabilitation	n.	恢复	09
reimbursable	a.	补偿的,偿还的	04

repay v. 偿还,还(钱等)		04
repayment n. 偿还;偿付的款项		04
repercussion n. 影响,反应;相互作用		15
repetitive * a. 重复的;反复的		16
replacement * n. 替换(物);补充		07
representation * n. 表示;描述;代表,代理		08
rethink n. 重新考虑		15
revenue * n. 收入,税收,收入总额		01
revolving fund 周转资金		04
roof v. 给…盖上屋顶,做…的屋面		10
roofing n. 屋面		13
rosy a. 乐观的,光明的;玫瑰色的		15
run up 欠下(许多债或账)		01
satisfy v. 说服,使相信,向……证实;使……满足		16
score n. 帐目;根据;理由		11
scrutinise v. 仔细检查;详审		15
sector n. (尤指商业,贸易等)部门,区域		09
sectoral a. 部分的,部门的;扇形的		10
set forth 宣布;发表		05
set out 制定,打算		07
setting out 设计;装饰,布置		13
shareholder n. 股东;股票持有人		15
short run 短期		09
short-term a. 短期的		10
simplistic a. 过分简单化的		09
site meeting n. 现场会		12
slab * n. 平板;厚片,厚板		13
slump n. 经济萧条;消沉;【商】(事业的)衰败;低落		06
specification * n. 说明书;(pl.)技术要求,规格		07
speculation n. 投机;思索,推测		14
speculator n. 投机者;思索者		14
spinal a. 脊柱的;脊髓的		13
stabilize,-ise * v. 稳定,安定		10
standardisation * n. 标准化,规格化		03

statement of changes in financial position 资金变动情况表,财务状况变动表		04
stock adjustment model 存量调整模型		09
strenuous a. 奋发的,使劲的		10
strife n. 竞争,冲突		01
strive v. 努力,力求;斗争		15
subcontract v. 转包工作,承做转包的工作		10
subcontractor n. 分包者,转包者		07
subsidize v. 资助,津贴,给……补助金		11
subunit n. 下属单位		11
suicide n. 自杀		01
summarization n. 概要,概述		11
superfouous a. 过多的;多余的		06
supervision n. 监督,管理		07
supplier * n. 供应厂商,供应者		07
susceptibility n. 敏感,感受性		09
susceptible * a. 易受影响的,敏感的		09
sustained a. 持久的,持续的,持久不变的		10
take account of 考虑……		03
take head 注意,提防,留意		12
tax shelter 减税		14
tender n.;v. 投标;提出		15
terminology n. 术语学,术语		09
the net result 最后结果		01
tie up 冻结,(资金)搁置,(使资金等)专做某用金而不能随便使用		04
timber * n. 木料;木材		02
timely a. 合时的,适时的,及时的		08
trade-off n. 交易,权衡		08
tradesman n. 手艺人;商人;店主		16
transition * n. 过渡(时期);转折		06
transpire v. 为人所知,泄漏;发散排出		15
transportable a. 可运输的,可移动的		03
trough n. 商业周期的低潮		09
turnover n. (工人)人员更新;翻倒,移交		10

twofold	a.	两重的,两件事的,两个部分的	08
ultimately	ad.	最终地;基本地	07
unaffordable	a.	无法得到的,无法达到的	01
unambiguous	a.	不含糊的,明确的	08
unanticipated	a.	不可预料的,无法预测的	07
understandable	a.	可懂的;可理解的	09
underutilize	v.	浪费地使用;对…未充分利用	13
uneconomical	a.	不经济的,浪费的	15
unforeseen	a.	预料不到的;事先不知道的	05
unionize	vt.	使成立联合组织;使成立工会	10
unsecured	n.	无抵押的,无担保的;没系牢的	14
update *	v.	使现代化	04
update *	v.	使现代化,更新	12
variability	n.	变化性;易变	09
variance *	n.	变化,变动,变异;方差	09
vary with	v.	随……而变化	09
verbal	a.	非书面的,言语的	12
verification *	n.	证据,证实	10
versus	prep.	与…相对(相比)	08
vice versa		反之亦然	08
warehouse *	n.	货栈,仓库	05
wattle	n.	枝条;篱笆条	02
weather	v.	【海】战胜(过渡)暴风雨;(喻)渡过	06
well—being	n.	福利	01
whilst	con j.	而;当……的时候	15
windfall	n.	被风吹落的果实(喻)轻易的收获,横财	01
wishful	a.	怀有希望的,表示愿望的	04
worklod	n.	(规定期限的)工作量;工作负担	06
workmanship	n.	手艺;技艺,工作质量	05
zero-sum	a.	一方得益引起另一方相应损失的	01

Appendix II   Translation for Reference

第 1 单元

何谓宏观经济学

宏观经济学所涉及的都是些大的经济问题，这些经济问题决定着你本人及你的家人和所有你知道的人的经济福利。其中的每一个问题都涉及一个国家整体的经济运行状况，而不是个人的经济情况。

比如说：公民觉得找工作是难还是易？一般说来，物价上涨得快还是慢，或是稳定不变？国民生产总值是多少？每年的总收入增长有多快？贷款的利率是高还是低？政府支出是否超过了税收？总的来说，国家在国外有资产积累还是有债务？

这六个问题无一不涉及到宏观经济的中心概念，这也是本课要向你介绍的内容。现在就让我们逐一探讨，看看他们是如何对日常生活产生影响的。

1. 失业率

整体失业率越高，个人找工作就越难。如果失业率低，毕业后需要找个稳定工作的在校四年级大学生可能有更多的就业机会。所有的成年人都惧怕高失业率，在失业率高的经济萧条时期，犯罪率上升，精神病患者增多，自杀现象也会增加，难怪许多人认为失业是唯一的最为重要的宏观经济问题，这已不是什么新鲜事。

2. 通货膨胀率

高通货膨胀率意味着物价普遍上涨迅速；低通货膨胀率意味着物价普遍上涨慢。通货膨胀率为零则意味着平均物价数月不变。在通货膨胀率由低变高时，许多人会受到影响。虽然高的通货膨胀率损害了那些存款者的利益，但是却让那些借贷者占了便宜。正是这种亏了部分人而便宜了另一部分人的反复无常的特性，使得人们讨厌通货膨胀。

3. 生产率的增长

生产率是指一个国家生产的商品和提供服务总量中每个工人的平均生产量。一个国家的平均生产水平越高，可供分配的物资就越多。平均生产率增长越快，社会成员的生活水平就越容易得到提高。假如生产率增长为零，我们又打算拥有更多的住房或汽车，那么必须作出牺牲，少建一些学校和医院。这种生产率不增长的经济叫做一方受益而另一方受损的经济。因为一个人多得到的商品或服务就会使另一个人少得到商品或服务。这样一个人们经常作出牺牲和不断地发生冲突的社会不可能是一个舒心的生活环境。

4. 利率

利率高时，借贷就昂贵，受损失最大的要算是那些打算买房的人了。因为高利率使每月交纳的抵压金一涨再涨，使许多购房者付不起款。在校大学生和刚毕业大学生觉得按月分期付款额太高，买新汽车的梦想难以实现。他们只好买小型汽车，二手车或不买车。利率的变化（不管是升还是降）影响着每个人的经济计划，会给那些存款者、投资者、借贷者带来意想不到的收获或损失。

5. 政府预算赤字

当政府支出超过税收时，则出现赤字。当出现预算赤字时人们可以从中得到好处，因为他们从政府高支出中得到的比收支平衡时得到的多。然而，这并非是"免费午餐"，因为最终还是要有人付帐。现在的赤字亏空一定要直接地或间接地由公民将来去填平，这其中包括正在阅读本文的在校生。公民最终要偿还政府的这笔债务。其方式只能是降低政府开支，提高税收或是减少公民收入。

6. 外贸赤字

在本世纪八十年代，美国进口的商品比出口商品多得多，为了支付这些进口的商品，美国把大量资产卖给外国人。到八十年代末，美国就欠下了上千亿美元的外债。这样一来，洋货更贵，下一代的公民更加贫穷，他们要把未来收入的一部分作为利息付给外国人。

第2单元

建筑经济（Ⅰ）

建筑业在任何经济体制中都是最重要的行业之一。一个国家大部分的资源通常都要用在建筑物的建造和维修上。建筑在生产和向社会提供服务方面都发挥着重要作用。显而易见，从所利用的资源上获得很好的效益是很重要的。建筑和建筑物常遭到批评不足为奇。不幸的是，大部分批评并无根据。而且常常把与建筑有关的许多复杂因素给忽视了。其结果是，许多批评性建议几乎没有多大价值，甚至带有破坏性。

许多产品，以及生产这些产品的行业只是近几十年才趋于完善，而当今人们所了解的建筑和建筑物却是在整个历史过程中不断发展起来的。他们的发展随着时间的推移，因地而异。树枝搭成的圆锥形小屋既是现代化建筑形式的雏形，又是当今世界上某些地区的建筑形式本身。过去，当普通百姓用泥、枝条和木头搭建的时候，教会和政府却用砖块和石料。很自然，只有一些具有纪念意义的供教会和政府使用的大型建筑至今硕果仅存。而那些普通老百姓居住的房舍则早已荡然无存，只在世界上一些不太发达民族当前居住的建筑物中才能看到。建筑物的发展史主要是研究一些国家过去和现在各种建筑形式和当时存在的各种条件之间的关系，这将有助于了解建筑经济中目前存在的问题。

在经济落后地区，普通老百姓自己建造房屋，而专业建筑商只被教会和政府部门所雇用。因而，住宅建筑和大型公用性建筑朝着不同方向发展。住宅建筑一般是由住户和其邻居就地取材而建造的。起初，所用的材料都是原始毛料。后来，人们渐渐地作出更大的努力对材料进行加工，以便住房结构楔合更好，形式更方便，更能防御风雨的侵袭。自然，那些偶尔为之的人不可能获得终身从事这一行业的那些人所具有的技能和知识。这一行当的技能代代相传，并在与其它地区同行们的接触过程中得以丰富。专业建筑的发展比住户自建建筑的发展要快得多。随着社会财富的增加和社会更加复杂化，原来满足于自己建造房屋的人们，以及有这方面的欲望和有时间来搭建及维修房屋的人，其比例正在缩小，越来越多的人雇用专业建筑工人。因此，建筑和建筑物的演变是建材、技能和外部经济相互作用的结果。

在很多方面，两千多年以来专业建筑并没有发生根本性的变化。罗马时代富翁们的住宅与现代的房屋没有什么两样，罗马时代的工程结构跟今天的一样宏大，一样引人注目。另一方面，现在可用的建筑材料范围要宽得多，对其性能的了解也更加深刻。因此，人们能够更加大胆而且经济地使用这些材料。此外，机械辅助施工的范围更加扩大，从而减少了所需的人力或时间。建筑方面最具意义的变化还在于当前工程技术服务的范围拓宽了。

发达国家大部分建筑工程都是专业建筑，而不发达国家的情况正好与此相反。自然，自建自住的房屋往往缺少西方国家家庭所期望的便利设施，尤其是机械和管道设备方面的。发展中国家所面临的经济问题就是选准时机，转变那种用当地的通常寿命较短的材料来建造自住房屋的做法，改成用机械加工材料的专业建筑方式。

在分工精细的社会里，普通老百姓通常找专业建筑工人来做主要的建筑工作，而次要的或维修工作则往往留后自己动手做。在劳动力价格的增长比原材料和构件的价格增长，以及税后净收入增长快的社会里，在构件的变损和廉价的小电动工具更容易买到，从而既降低了技术要求，又降低了劳动强度的社会里，这种情况呈增长趋势。

第3单元

效　　率

建筑业的效率和由此而产生的建筑成本取决于以下五种因素：业主、设计师、承包商、材料制造商和经济、社会环境。业主的作用是在动手设计之前能够详细地说明其需要和对设计人员提出的方案进行评价。设计师起着核心作用，他们的贡献主要表现在能拿出建造和使用都省费用的方案以满足业主的需要，为此，他必需考虑到施工过程中很可能出现的问题以及能获取和生产所用材料和构件的程度。设计师对建筑成本的影响比承包商或是材料制造商都要大，因为他们可以确定整个建筑，他们不仅可以通过充分利用材料和简化施工过程的方式来降低造价，而且还可以通过设计，以较小的空间，并以最小的墙体和屋顶面积将此空间包围起来，以满足需要。承包商对降低造价所能起到的作用是他们的建造效率。这不仅是个速度问题还是一个劳力和组织之间的协调问题。材料制造商的作用是通过提高采掘、制造和材料部件的分送过程的效率来降低产品的价格。经济和社会环境对效率的影响主要是通过为设计和施工提供方便和为建筑业所制订的各项规章来实现。

绝大部分业主只是偶尔地发挥其作用，并在很大程度上要依靠设计师的业务能力来确定业主需要的性质和提出的方案的价值。

建筑设计，尤其是今天，是个极为复杂的问题，比起其它设计来，需要更加广博的知识。这种复杂性主要是由下面几个方面所引起的：建筑物的大小和功能的多少；所能提供服务的数量及范围；材料范围和可采用的施工方法等。设计上节省只能通过对使用者的基本要求的理解程度和对许多可行方案最终造价结果的比较能力来达到。一幢建筑的各部分的设计相互关联，也与该建筑的用途密切相连，且影响着其经营和内部使用费用。因此，谁都不可能在建筑设计和业务的各个方面成为样样精通的专家，但是，设计组的领导必须至少对各方面出现的问题能够有一个总的了解。

新的建筑材料和新的建筑工艺的发展以及建筑所能提供的服务功能更加复杂化，给建筑施工及设计增添了难度。还在不久以前，建材选用范围和建筑技术还很有限，建筑工人根据所提供的简单轮廓图样的资料便可着手建造。配套的服务设施少且简单，承包商通常了解整个建造过程。如今，建筑类型很广，许多服务设施非常复杂，所以详尽的图纸和专业知识是必不可少的。传统的工匠起的作用减少了，雇用的专业工人越来越多，建筑形式更为复杂，建筑速度要求更快，这使得有必要认真做好施工现场规划和组织。常规的施工方式已不再适用。此外，生活水平和总的工作条件的改善，加之许多发达国家的劳动力越来越短缺，就需要更好的组织，更好的劳动环境和更高的劳动报酬。工人劳动力的费用越高就越需要提高劳动力的使用效率。

传统的建材一般是粗大，笨重且形状和大小不一。它们的价格本身虽然便宜，但用起来却很昂贵。这些材料的使用技术已有了改进。即使如此，这些材料的技术性能仍很有限。此外，由于粗大，笨重，运费很高。在运输条件相当落后的年代或在情况仍然如此的国家里，使用的建材大部分都是当地的，外地材料一般不多用。由于条件所限，建筑形式也受到了限制，建筑费用也相当高。价格低廉的交通运输的发展导致了建材价格的下降，可用的建材品种的增加。这样，既促进了现有材料的推广和标准化，又促进了那些便于运输的建材的发展。出现了一些新材料，其中一些往往是在其它领域研制出来的。它们比传统的材料使用起来更方便，重量更轻，规格也更统一。这样的材料常使很多难题得以解决，就用途而言也比传统材料便宜。不过新材料常常不易同传统材料结合在一起用。

第4单元

现 金 预 测

进行现金预测，通常有必要按月来估算一下什么时候可以得到施工分期付款以及什么时候可通过别的渠道弄到现金。在此基础上，对财务状况变动情况的预测有时是有用的。在进行现金预测时，有必要提前预测已知工作费用、企业管理费用、税收、设备购置及还贷费用的现金需求。

有些承包商认为这种预测是浪费时间，因为由于款项的回收不可预测，在完成现金预测之前，这种预测就已过时了，而且还因为这种预测会错误引导看预测报告的人，使他们提前使用手头没有的资金。所有这些反对意见都没有言中要害。这类现金预测要做到如下两点。第一，这种预测要列出现金来源的清单，并要平衡预期需求与现存资金的关系。第二，这种预测要把该做的工作以及如果手头要有款付帐时该收进的款项列入计划表。

一些建筑公司所用的现金预测做起来是很快的，因为他们不求预测极其准确。然而预测必须得由了解情况、知晓预测目的的人来做，要制定一个尽可能切合实际并在必要时可以更新的财经计划。在此基础上就可能估算出需要什么样的短期贷款以及用什么方式，什么时间去偿还这些贷款。有了这种提供给银行家的预测，需要借贷者就可很容易地借到所需贷款。如果有理由认为预计资金的收款速度会减慢的话，这种预测就会告诉我们，有必要在收款方面作出更大的努力。

在对一个新的业务的估算方式上，预计可得到的现金可能会有很大的差别。如果有足够的业务资金，承包商可能会对更多的总额承包工程投标。如果业务资金有可能一度周转困难的话，承包商可能试图将一些总额承包标位转为由业主提供周转资金运转的补偿性的成本加成费用工程。如果业务量少以及正在进行的工程快要完成时，承包商可能更加激烈地去竞标，而且在预知能够从完成的工程中得到资金为新工程筹措资金时便会以较低的盈利去竞标。

有些现金预测是基于业务的种类，而不是单项的作业。因此，收方科目可能是"合同业务"、"维护业务"、"修理业务"等等。用于支出的项目可能是"工资支出"、"进货支出"、"税务支出"。在有些建筑业务中，这是一种唯一可行的办法。

在使用这些预测时，有三种主要的局限性：其一，预测没有所设想的那么准确。所以这种预测不是可以交给随便什么人做的一种数字游戏。它是对刚过去月份的一个月度总结和即将来临的月份的经营项目的最佳估算。在预测准备期间，公司管理层及其聘用的会计和财务顾问一起集思广益，共同考虑公司当前的各种财务问题。如果现金预测不以这种方式来进行，预测就会失去很多其本该有的意义。实际上，有可能成为一些批评者所指控的那样把人引入歧途。

其二，必须记住的是，这种预测不能担保任何事情。只有基于这种预测的想法变成实际行动时，资金才有望到位。特别是在需要银行贷款时，有一种很强的诱惑力使人沉溺于一厢情愿的思考和过于乐观的猜测中。这可能偶尔行得通，但如果数额证实不合情理时，银行业者就会怀疑承包商的所有预测。这对信誉来说是最为有害的。鉴于银行同保险公司之间工作往来关系密切，这也可能对承包商接受担保能力的信誉带来危害。现金预测象投标一样要求冷静，过分的乐观都会带来严重的麻烦。相反，细致、谨慎的预测是财务管理中最为有效的工具之一。

其三，现金预测并不一定预示着获利或损失。一个承包商可能在做大量的高利润业务且仍然缺少现金。实事上，承包商经常处于这种境地。不断扩大的业务使资金很难运转。营运资金存放在银行帐户上的时间不会比生产设备停放在承包商院子里的时间长。为了做出税收计划和长期经营计划，合适的做法是进行"损益"或"经营"预测。

第 5 单元

成功的投标方案

　　成功的投标方案一般是按既定方式提交的。此例中业主要求当地的两家建筑公司提交投标方案，业主对方案进行评估后从中选定了最符合该项目要求的专业化建筑管理方案。
　　下文便是成功的建筑管理（CM）投标方案的摘要。方案是以一封信函的形式提交的，信中概述了计划提供的各项服务，而且对总公司在提供服务时所需的固定费用以及一般间接费用和利润给予了报价。

　　建筑管理与控制有限公司关于简易干货储备仓库的建筑管理方案（1984年9月1日）
　　　　　　　　案第　84—17号
交：彼得·J·柯利弗兰先生
　　方便食品公司设计与建筑部经理
　　美国西部山城（邮区号99999）麦迪逊大街200号
题目：山城干货储备仓库的专业化建筑管理方案
亲爱的柯利弗兰先生：
　　应您的要求本公司很高兴为建筑山城干货储备仓库呈上关于提供专业化建筑管理服务的方案。
　　建筑管理与控制有限公司计划提供一种旨在维护固定价格建筑承包合同的利益的同时能实现仓库在十个月后竣工的目标的管理服务方案。通过运用"快轨"法（或分期施工法），进行固定价格建筑承包合同的拟定、招标和签授等工作，确保楼房尽早完工，以便能够在冬季继续进行内部装修保证在明年春季如期交付业主使用。
　　在此本公司计划将提供下列服务：
　　1. 准备管理规划：准备一份管理规划总表，列有经反复考虑后的有关投标的一揽子方案和实现工程目标所需的施工期限。
　　2. 制定投标的一揽子方案：在业主和建筑师的协助下，制定一系列各种详细的投标一揽子方案，这些方案应适应于一次性付清款项的投标。
　　3. 准备投标人入选名单：对具有完成该项工作所应具备的专业技能的、有希望的投标人进行资格预审工作。
　　4. 准备公允的造价预算：为每项投标方案提交一份公允的造价预算表，以备评估投标方案时使用。
　　5. 接受、审查和评估投标方案：主持投标的开标仪式，对投标方案进行评估，并且为方便食品公司进行合同的裁定提供推荐书。
　　6. 管理、协调、检查工作：依本公司之见方便食品有限公司的代表将定期视察工作并且建筑师也将按要求对工程进行定期检查。本公司（建筑管理与控制有限公司）将指派一名专职的施工现场主管到工地管理、协调与监督工程的所有正在进行的工作，他的职责将包括：协调各类合同；控制各个阶段的施工进度；为协调工作提出建议，以顺应不断变化和没有预料到的一些情况；拟写工程进度报告；对施工分期付款情况进行检查并且提出建议；获得所需要的现场工作图并将其转交给建筑师以获批准；按要求征得实验室所提供的检验服务；检查材料的质量和工艺质量；做好工程日志及其它的记录；为了使工程的进行与业主要求一致，做好其它一些常规要求的服务工作。

7. 由总公司提供协助服务：建筑管理与控制有限公司将从总公司指派一名负责协助业主的项目经理，参与所有工作并为了此目的在所需的范围里"按需"使用他。除此之外，本公司备有一份本公司的管理及技术人才资料表以备整个工程中出现特殊需求时供业主参考。

如果所有的现场费用都计算在内的话，我们提供的专业建筑管理服务为固定的费用其中包括总公司的服务费，这一固定费用为十万美元。

我们的方案还须经双方协商达成彼此都满意的协议。

我们极为珍惜此次机会能向贵公司山城项目的专业建筑管理服务提出本公司的投标方案，由于我们的方案只是基于提供初步信息，我们十分愿意就计划做进一步的探讨，如果需要的话，纳入修改意见，以便与贵方的总目标更加符合。

你忠实的
建筑管理与控制有限
公司总裁
J·沃尔特·哈里顿

第 6 单元

建筑是个变化无常的行业

危机

任何一个行业都不可能原地踏步或者没有危机。危机通常是由合伙人无法控制的外部事件引起的。合伙人所能做的就是拿出对策，采取措施，以减少损失或有可能的话在所面临的环境中去获利。

由内部因素引起的危机则属于另一种性质。此类危机可能是由于内部人员之间的关系长期处于紧张或不和状态，最终发展到再也无法维持的严重地步所致，高层人员的调动也可能引起大的混乱，从而影响了企业的服务质量。

从许多方面看，这些危机与国内、国外的经济繁荣期及萧条期所带来的后果相比都是微不足道的。那么，经济的繁荣与萧条期是如何影响建筑师的业务经营的呢？现在就让我们来看看繁荣期，萧条期以及由繁荣转向萧条，又由萧条走向繁荣的各个时期的特点吧。

萧条

本世纪曾出现过两次明显的萧条期，一次是从本世纪20年代末至30年代初，另一次则是从本世纪70年代中期到80年代初。政府经费的削减，尤其是对资金需要量大的工程项目的削减是引起建筑业衰退、进而造成建筑师失业的直接原因。这一结果首先是引起股市和利率的变更，消费水平的降低导致了工厂的倒闭和大批失业群的产生。那么，首先采用的应急对策就是削减资本开支，而这些经费正是我们这一行业的命脉。

繁荣

近20年来，最为明显的兴盛期出现在1970年至1973年期间，当时政府认为，通过增加货币的投放量和鼓励私有企业的发展可以促进经济繁荣。

繁荣期呈现后人们往往能感觉到，人们的商务活动增加，设计师办公室开始接到更多的工作并且打算进一步扩展。这是一个令人感到安全、兴奋、让人充满信心和成就感的时期，不过囿于我们这个社会的本质，繁荣期一般不会持续很长时间。

从繁荣走向萧条

这种过渡期是最痛苦的，需要极高的技巧去应付。

过渡期第一个明显的迹象是工作减少，职员不得不被解雇。它常常是个痛苦而艰难的过程。涉及房产的各种问题及现金流量突然下降，设备过剩，整个行业的大改组都是这一过程的组成部分。通常，在繁荣时期即将结束时，仍然有相当多的在建项目，资金也仍不断地流入，还有一定的后劲。不过，到办公室来签约的项目明显地减少了。

资金还要用在繁荣时期承接的项目中未完成的工程上，但不祥之兆已显露了出来，因此不得不对各种削减做出安排。任何一个办公室最宝贵的资源要算是职员了，而且这也是首先要应付的任务。由于经理们和合伙人们对在其手下工作的职员们的工作效率意见不同，所以，决定解雇老的雇员而留用新来的充满前途的职员是个很痛苦又极困难的事。

削减繁荣时期能负担得起的一些多余的设施往往会明显地影响职工的士气，当办公地点缩小后，所有的人都要开始在更加有限的空间里与新的工作班子一起工作的时候尤其影响职工的士气。因此，当此类变化发生后，人员四散，工资扯平了，晋升机会更少，工作更具竞争性，设计费降低了，工作单位的内部竞争也加剧了。这就可能要求用极高的经营技巧去平息这场风暴，而不至于受任何损伤，以便在经济衰退中也能谋利，并为注定要来临的回升期做好准备。

从萧条走向繁荣

如果你度过了衰退期，而且生意正逐渐好转，那么，这时要做的工作增多，钱更容易借贷，经营上也有一个乐观的经济基础，人们也不再因超负荷地工作而显得精疲力尽。

业务增多时，首先碰到的难题是你是否拥有充足的资金来保障你经营的业务开展下去。你可以去找银行经理多筹借些资金，而此时在总的经济领域里他们的许多客户尚处在不能自拔的衰退之中或刚缓过劲儿来，这就意味着你必须极具说服力并对你的预测的正确性充满信心，以便能为你的事业发展筹集更多的资金。也许，最艰巨的任务就是使你的资金提供者们相信现在的投资将来必定挣得更大的利润。

事业的扩展，仍需要增添办公场所。而此时正是你准备集中精力抓好新的工作的时候，这就不能不给你带来很多麻烦和纠纷。办公场所的租用或者购置并装修办公场所都是很费钱的，而这时候，办公室里纷至沓来的工程项目合同也需要资金投入，其结果是，尽管项目应接不暇，但你会面临资金周转困难的麻烦，而且不得不借中期贷款或要求业主按月付款。从整体上看，这样做有可能使利润降低，但能保证在业务扩展起来时有足够的周转资金。在此期间你也必须记住：走向繁荣的过渡期最终会导致走向繁荣期的过渡，弄不好，又会走向衰退。而几年过后你又可能重新回到了你刚开始的那种业务状况。

第 7 单元

谁需要质量保证

> 一种材料，一件产品，一项服务必须符合规定的要求，质量保证（QA）就是为其增加信誉的管理体系。

建筑方面的业主会理所当然地问他为什么要为质量保证费神呢？质量保证似乎对那些向消费者销售商品的厂家（如豹牌汽车生产商、马克斯·斯宾塞连锁商场）更加有用。不管怎样，工程是会按他的要求设计的，承包人根据合同，也必须按照设计图纸和技术要求完成建筑工程，这些都是可以通过法律得以实施的。

不幸的是，正如许多业主付出了惨重的代价后才明白的那样，建筑的完成并不像上述的那样简单，合乎法律的合同即使签订后也并不能保证业主最终可获得称心如意的竣工工程。尽管业主通过仲裁机构或民事法庭的判决得到赔偿，但他同样也不会感到宽慰。业主也不可能像马克斯·斯宾塞商场的顾客那样再去换一样称心的商品，留给他的只能是拼凑起来的原物，很可能会令人烦恼不断，成为一个填不满的钱坑。

不称心建筑溯源

那么，造成令人不满意的建筑的根源何在呢？首要的，也是最为关键的因素是团体与人。所谓团体，我们指的是业主和那些与他直接或间接签有合同关系的人。这批人合计起来数量相当可观，其中包括主要设计师、专家顾问团、承包商、分包商以及产品和材料供应商。

说到人，我们这里指的是那些签订了合同的团体内部的设计人员和施工人员，以及那些在此过程中必须发生联系的人们。这些人所造成的麻烦就在于他们在相互交流中普遍带有不准确性，这种不准确性发生在技术事务的交流中的程度并不亚于日常聊天。将人数乘以他们在完成工程中必须交流的次数，所获得的潜在引起误会与误解的机会次数将是很大的。

过失分析

什么是过失？潜在的原因又是什么呢？

建筑科学研究中心通过对一些过失进行分析后认为，绝大多数过失是由设计错误和施工质量低引起的，可能仅仅只有10%是由于用材不当所致。

设计错误的原因可能包括：
1. 对业主需求的误解。
2. 使用了不正确或过时的信息。
3. 对设计标准的误解。
4. 各类设计师之间缺乏交流。
5. 所提供的技术要求不充分，不准确。

施工中出现失误的原因有：
1. 对设计图纸和技术要求的误解。
2. 与供应商和分包商缺乏交流。
3. 各分包工作之间缺乏协调。
4. 因指挥不当造成施工质量低下。
5. 施工现场监督不力。

如何争取"一次"成功？

业主若想一次就能获取合格工程，他可以采取以下三个主要的措施：
1. 积极参与此项工程；
2. 做到系统化；
3. 要求承包商也做到系统化。

业主必须从以下几个方面参与此项工程：
1. 从一开始就准确地说明自己的需求（关键是对主要设计师说明）；
2. 认真挑选承包团体；
3. 保证责任明确。

若想使这些任务得到有效地执行，业主在其努力争取的过程中必须要采取系统化的方法。不过，既然业主做到了工作系统化，那么，承包方为何不照此办理呢？做到这一点的方法是要求他们运用质量保证法。

运用质保（QA）：

一种材料，一件产品或一项服务必须符合规定的要求，质量保证的目的就是提高这方面的信誉。就建造过程来说，业主应把这些要求向主设计师讲清楚。

如果供应商要运用质量保证的话，他就必须在一个质量体系内工作。简而言之，质量体系是关于对供应商的正常工作方式的书面描述，以保证供应商提供的材料、产品或服务的质量。实质上，除了制定供应商工作时应符合的标准外，质量体系还讲述了如何达到这些标准的方法。按照这些质量体系行事，供应商就更有可能一次性使其产品合格。

质量保证的益处和含义：

对于业主来说，质量保证的主要益处是它能使自己有更强的信心认为他的工程将：

1. 按期竣工；
2. 符合业主要求；
3. 不超预算。

此外，还要对如下三个方面给予适当的重视。

质量保证的主要含义是业主必须：
1. 在其工程上投入更多的时间；
2. 承认有必要做到自身工作系统化；
3. 承担任何额外的初始费用。

权衡利弊后，业主应该不惜任何额外的初始费用，用以减少完工后的工程出现以下风险：
1. 工期延误——伴随而来的资金损失；
2. 不令人满意——可能需另拨款加以修正；
3. 超过预算。

此外，业主可以参考那些已发现质量保证能节省成本的人们所获得的经验。这些人已逐渐领悟到支持建筑合同的人与系统和建筑合同是同等重要的。

第8单元

管理会计在决策中的作用

管理会计在决策过程中的职责是向作决定的经理们提供有关的信息。生产经理通常要对可供选择的生产过程和生产计划作出决定，市场行销经理进行价格决策，财务方面的专家们则常常要对一些重要的设备购置问题作出决策。所有这些经理们都需要与决策相关的信息，因此，管理会计需要充分了解经理们所面临的决策问题。

决策步骤：

1. 弄清决策问题：有时需要进行决策的问题很清楚，例如：某公司收到一份要求低于正常价格条件下购买其产品的订货单，那么决策问题就是接受或拒绝这份订单。但是，决策问题却很少如此清晰明了，或许对某公司最畅销产品的需求正在减少，到底是什么原因呢？因此在做出决策之前必须对需要决策的问题了解清楚，并且作出具体说明。

2. 指定标准：一旦弄清了决策问题，经理们就应该规定进行决策的基本标准。决策的目的是什么呢？是尽量提高利润，提高市场的占有率？尽量降低成本？还是提高产品服务的质量？有时目标间会发生冲突，比如在决策中既要尽可能降低生产成本，又要保证产品质量，在这种情况下，其中一个目标将被指定为决策标准——如尽可能降低成本；而另一个目标则成为一项制约条件——如产品质量，一千个产品中最多允许一件次品。

3. 鉴定选择方案：决策时必然要在两个或更多的选择方案中进行选择。例如机器出了故障,有哪些可供选择的补救措施呢?机器可以修理,可以替换,还可能租借一台机器。在决策过程中决定可供选择的一些方案是很关键的一步。

4. 建立决策模型:决策模型就是对被选择的问题所作的一份简明扼要的描述。所以,决策模型包括了以上列举的一些因素、标准、限制条件和选择方案。

5. 收集数据资料:选择与决策有关的数据资料是管理会计在一个组织中所担负的最重要的职责之一。

6. 选择一项方案:一旦决策模型形成,相关数据收集完成后,主管经理就可以做出决定了。

定量与定性分析

决策问题中所包含的会计性资料常常用数量语汇加以说明,然而当经理做出最后决定时选择方案的定性特征与定量测试对他同样重要。定性特征是决策问题中无法用数字表达清楚的一些因素。为了说明两者之间的区别,让我们假设:环球航空公司的高层管理人员正在考虑关闭伦敦中枢站。经过详细的定量分析后表明最大限度提高环球航空公司利润的一项选择方案就是关闭伦敦中枢站,然而在决定过程中公司的经理们将考虑到许多有关定性的问题,诸如关闭后对伦敦站下属雇员们的影响以及对公司所属的巴黎、亚特兰大、东京各站的留任的雇员们士气的影响。

为了弄清楚在这种定性分析中的利害悠关的因素、定量分析可使决策人员将定性特征所带来的价值总额进行"标价",比如环球航空公司的总会计师向高层管理人员递交了一份定量分析报告,它表明伦敦中枢站的关闭将会给公司每年增加 2,000,000 美元的利润。然而考虑到定性因素伦敦站继续运行为好。这些定性因素对高层管理者们来说究竟有多重要呢?如果他们决定继续让伦敦站运行,这些定性因素对他们来说起码要值 2,000,000 美元。所以在决策中权衡定量与定性因素是管理的最重要的方面。

获得信息:相关性,精确性,及时性

管理会计在设计决策信息系统中应该使用何种标准呢?信息的三个特征决定其有效性。

相关性:如果信息与决策问题有关联,那么它就具有相关性。

精确性:与决策问题相关的信息也必须是准确的,否则它就没有丝毫价值。这意味着信息必须精确。然而十分准确但无关的资料对决策者来说也是没有价值的。

及时性:相关的准确的信息资料只有是及时的才有价值。也就是说能够在做出决定前及时地获得这些信息。因此,及时性是决定信息的有效性的第三个重要标准。有些情况下会出现在信息的精确性和及时性之间进行权衡决择,越精确的信息收集起来花费的时间则越长,所以当精确性增加时,及时性则减少,反之亦然。

总而言之:管理会计在决策过程中的主要作用体现在两方面:

1. 确定与每个决策问题相关的信息是什么。
2. 提供准确及时的数据资料,牢记在这些常常发生冲突的标准之间保持适当的平衡。

第 9 单元

住 房 供 给

定义

在任何围绕着供给市场体系而进行的经济分析中，价格因素在调节供需双方的消费和生产计划方面起着至关重要的作用。因此，在考察住房供给体制中供房一方的时候，使人最感兴趣的是市场上所提供的住房交易量怎样随着房价变化而变化。这里不妨暂以与交易量有关的住房供应定义为题来谈谈。很显然，新提供的住房进入市场的速度随着新住房竣工速度而变；或随着现存住房中的住房交易量上升或下降而变。因此，即使住房供给这个简单的定义，也可能存在很复杂的现象。因为新房经销商和现房经销商都面临着不同的销售技术和计算价格等问题，即对新提供的住房和改建后的住房供应量都需要进行既互相区别，又相互联系的分析。此外，既然住房供求信息不可避免地反映出决策的履行效果和工程滞后的情况。那么，对住房供应量调节进行分析的时间周期也必须加以考虑。在传统的微观经济术语中市场周期的定义是：流通稳定期。在短期经营中供应量的一些可变因素可以有所变动，而在长期经营活动中，按其定义来看其投入和产出都可以有变化。因此"住房供给"这个普通术语本身并非特别有用，应该在特定时期内对某些供应部门加以分析才有意义。尽管住房供应最理想的概念模式可能与任一时期新提供的和以前存有的住房交易量相关。但是，这样的流通和流通中的调整模型怎样能明确表示出来和接受检验却难以想象。通常住房供给分析是利用存量调整模型来进行的，该模型主要涉及新住房量的加入，住房改建和改造的速度，以及从另一个极端看，还涉及住房的拆除以及住房折旧等方面的因素。

建筑部门经济

英国经济学家一向对住宅建筑问题感兴趣。不过这种兴趣一般只涉及国民经济中的宏观经济模式。而对城市经济学中所述的房屋改造、修复、流通调节及供应调节还没有进行系统的经济分析。不过正如下面将要阐述的那样，北美在城市住房市场的供给方面所作的经验总结和理论研究已取得相当可观的成果。而在英国，即使有人认为住房市场供应行为的微观经济基础研究本身是很重要的，但这种人也是为数甚少的。

宏观经济意义

考虑到建筑部门的规模和易受周期性影响等特点，人们对在建筑活动中需求产生的总的影响采取过分简单的态度也就在情理之中了。1976 年，英国的建筑部门的产量是国内总产值的 15%，雇用了约 250 万雇员。据估计住房建筑占建筑业总产出的三分之一。

建筑业对中央和地方的政策举措极为敏感，反映在公共事业方面的开支削减或限额的财政紧缩通常迅速影响着公共部门的建房积极性，在英国，公、私部门一般都是同时启动的（见表 9-1）。由于建筑活动所需资金几乎全部依赖于银行贷款，因此，贷款利率微小的上调就会对建筑业产生明显而又迅速的影响，对建筑业规模及其周期特性的观察结果最近在英国得到了证实，它们和在美国观察所得的模式略有不同。1975年以前的一段时期，英国的建筑周期模式与整体经济中总的资本构成模式在细节上有很大的不同。英国的建筑周期在经济衰退阶段，对利率的下调反应十分迅速，比其它主要周期提前大约一年的时间。经济活动处在上升趋势时，建筑周期的变化很不一致，起伏波动很明显。

住房工程的动工、竣工滞后及完工量上下波动情况见表9-1。很显然，在70年代早期住房产量达到创记录的水平后，70年代末期的住宅建筑出现了明显的衰减期。这一段显著的周期性特点反映了经济政策与具体的生产过程、投入以及建筑业内部决策机构之间的相互作用。与此同时，产量上的这一波动（或称为"走走停停"）形成了这样一种环境，使建筑决策者们必须在这种环境中经营，所产生的不稳定因素无疑影响着该时期的发展并会产生反作用。在我们的探讨即将转入对建筑业以及后来对公司各部门的微观经济进行展望时，必须记住这些影响。

第10单元

建 造

建筑工程实际建造期可能需要1~4年。建筑公司常把这一完成速率当作一个变量，根据需求情况的变化加以调整。如上所述，在需求旺季时，可通过加班加点等形式来加快进度，以确保房屋迅速出售。而在房屋市场疲软时，降低单位时间内的劳力投入，可以使工程进度放慢，从而避免建筑商因存有未售空房而花费额外的管护及财政费用。

显然，建筑公司需要具有多方面的管理技能，以便在工程开工时，能有效地进入施工阶段。但在实际组织施工之前，还需作出相当大的努力，分阶段地完成一系列的小型合同项目。表10-1列出了建造一幢房子所需的各种技术工种的需求量，而这些常常由小型分包商提供。这种大量的小规模投入，说明了劳工使用中的低效和不可分割性可能是该产业的一个典型问题。这种复杂性在一些要求现场施工的特殊阶段里表现更为突出。如施工中期主要需要构架工人在工地操作。不难看出，一位手里有许多需要在不同阶段完工的大型建筑工地的指挥者，在具体的劳力投入方面，比起小型建筑商更具有系统性。一些小公司，实际上还包括许多稍大些的公司，都要通过签订大量的短期分包合同，来克服由于所需技术的变更而产生对不同技能工人的需求问题。但在这种情况下，通过签订大量的小型分包合同而获得的劳动力使用效率，必然要以增加建筑生产的困难和推迟建筑生产的时间为代价来换取。在非集团性的小型公司里如果雇员具有多种不同的技能，则可以克服这些阶段性的困难。例如：普工、细木工、瓦工、装饰工这些在集团公司中需要具有专门技术工人做的工作，在小型公司中则可能由同一批工人来承担。

劳务市场

前面已经提到，在建筑施工中，要求各个工种的配合，不同施工阶段各种劳力投入的情况也非常复杂,因而也就出现了在建筑行业中如何提高效率的问题。这里强调的是效率问题,特别是效率工资。显然持续的工资增长对建造业的计划及管理提出特殊要求,因为该产业生产力增长低,而且在实际生产过程中,又不可能相应地减少劳力投入。

建房工程中低生产率增长早已在英国引起关注,并且也是其他国家经济界评论的话题。这一问题不同程度地归因于管理水平低,未能在设计阶段引进先进的技术以及劳动力大量流动的这种传统管理方式。这些议论似乎有道理,但缺乏详细的经验上的例证。

20世纪70年代的通货膨胀使得劳动生产率问题具有特殊意义。建筑部门工资统计显示:该部门工资增长率到1977年已接近了全国的平均水平,尽管最近的情况表明建筑部门工资远低于全国水平。总的说来,建筑行业每周工作时数已超过平均工作时间。而工业生产指数说明建筑部门中人均产出量落后于全国平均水平。当然,由于劳动者技能低下,这种人均低产出率是不可能上升的。而且土地条件的好坏、使用资金的多少和管理水平的高低都会影响每个人(每台机器、每英亩)的平均产量。人们已做出很大的努力寻找提高建筑业生产率的途径,特别是非现场批量生产建筑构件,被认为是提高生产率的一个途径,虽然提高幅度有限。然而,斯坦格曼引用关于部门不平衡增长的鲍莫尔模型,对美国在70年代提高该业的生产率并不乐观。

建筑业是劳动力投入十分重要的一个产业。因此,在协议工资占相当比重的时代,如果建筑业的工资增长幅度高于其生产效率,房价必然上涨。而且,至少在美国,非现场生产的劳力投入也达到了极限,不可能以进一步提高劳动生产率来稳定房屋价格。标准化住房的增加也不受潜在消费者的欢迎,因为他们实际收入不断增长,更加希望住房多样化。

由于建筑业失业率快速增长,且呈周期性,目前英国的建筑业工资已远远落后于全国工资走向。只好希望目前的这种衰退不会引发淘汰体力劳动,摒弃该行业各种技能,废弃那些目前搁置不用的固定设备。

第11单元

会 计

会计学:富有活力的学科

会计学涉及财务数据的收集、总结和报告等方面。会计学是一个富有活力的学科,其中新的规则,新的程序不断产生。这篇文章的目的就是向读者(主要是现在和未来的经理以及投资人)提供必要的知识和技能,以充分利用会计资料。在做计划、控制及评估各部门工作以及在作个人或公司投资决策时,他们应该会利用会计资料。经理和投资人不仅应该意识到财务报告能提供大量信息,而且同样重要的是,他们也应该认识到这些信息的局限性。至少他们应该清楚什么时候向会计专家请教,问些本行业务中该问的问题。

会计的目标

　　会计工作包括对各种经济活动的说明，对经济价值的衡量以及测定这些经济价值的周期性变化。会计工作旨在为几个主要目标提供信息，其中有：

　　1. 对我们这个社会很有限的资源进行分配。在任何一种经济体制下，无论是资本主义还是社会主义，关于资金的投向决策都是基于金融报表提供的信息制定的。在自由开放的企业体制里，个人投资商购买企业股票，主要是根据企业阶段性盈利报告。银行家以及其他投资人在作出贷款决策前，也要研究对方的财务报告。政府有关部门决定向谁抽税，给谁补贴依据的也是财务报告。

　　2. 在一个企业里管理并指导资源的使用。无论是盈利还是非盈利实体的经理都一样依靠会计账目来确保其对人力，物力的有效管理，以及确保这些资源用于他们企业里最具有生产效率的产品、下属企业或部门。

　　3. 根据个人或组织的要求报告资源的掌管情况：个人，无论是作为投资者或仅仅是一般公民都委托那些职业经理和政府官员来管理资源。他们希望这些经理或政府官员能提供阶段性的报告，以此来对职业经理和政府官员的工作情况进行评估。

着重未来

　　会计工作着重对广泛的财务数据进行测定和传递。会计人员提供用以制定资金投放决策所需的资料。一旦决策制定出，他们要提供能够有效地管理这些资金所需的数据。当这一管理过程实施时，会计人员要阶段性地"公布账目"——提供情况以评估先前决策所产生的效果。

　　从略微不同的观点看，会计的目的在于使经理、投资商、债权人以及其他需用金融报表的人能够判断出企业将来的盈利能力。今天作出的决策只能影响到将来，而对过去无效。从金融报表中找信息的人所关心的主要是企业未来几年的前景而不是已经过去的情况。

　　然而，将来会发生的情况完全能从过去的情况中预见到。未来几年企业的管理能力最容易通过查阅前几年的财务档案而作出预测。

财务会计与管理会计

　　财务会计与管理会计之间通常是有区别的。财务会计是向企业外部的各方提供报表，管理会计则是提供企业内部需用的财务数据。

　　财务会计主要是给投资者以及潜在投资者提供信息。在对外部报告时，该企业必须坚持一般公认的会计原则。这些原则融法规制度与长期形成的习惯为一体，才有助于确保报告具有与其他企业的报告的可比性、在时间上的一致性和非故意地出现误差或误导。

　　管理会计给内部人员（董事长、经理及雇员）提供所需信息。它提供的信息用于制定企业工作目标，制定完成这些目标的策略和计划，管理企业的日常活动，并且阶段性地评估企业在完成其目标过程中所取得的进展。当该企业给内部人员发布报告时，报告不必满足于外界规定的标准，或恪守特定的会计原则。

第 12 单元

承包商的职责

（有关工程延期部分）

承包商的职责就是承包商必须遵守的细则。

一旦承包商认为工程受到延误或有可能被延误时，就必须立即书面通知业主。口头通知或记录在经双方同意的现场会议的通知都是不够的。通知必须包括延误的理由，如果有造成工期延误的理由，就须根据自己的看法，说明哪一种是直接相关的。

承包商应尽早给出相关事件预期结果的详细说明。

承包商必须尽快地估计出超出合同竣工期的延误时间是多少，并且分别写出对每一个有关事件的影响，说明这些延误会不会同时发生。如果估计对工程的竣工期不会造成全面的延误，他必须向业主如实报告。

如果承包商提到指定的分包商，他必须将书面通知的复印件，包括详细情况及延期的估计递交有关的分包商。

必要时，或根据业主的要求，承包商必须不时地进一步通知业主最新的延误详情并告诉业主估计延误会对竣工日期带来什么影响。承包商必须把每一份最新报告的复印件送给所有接到过第一份通知的指定分包商。承包商有责任在整个合同期间，不断报告延误的情况直到工程实际完工。如果没有做到这一点，他将陷入违反合同的境地，另外还会严重影响他获得任何延长工期的机会。

承包商提供他所掌握的信息，也是为了自己的利益。他必须认真将通知以文件形式送交业主。并且对业主关于提供进一步信息的要求，及时给予答复。实际上，承包商是在努力为自己的境况争辨。

除了给业主书面通知外，承包商还有两项责任：

他必须不断地尽其所能在工程进展中防止延误，并防止或减少对竣工期的任何影响。这并不意味着他必须花钱来弥补延误带来的损失，而是他必须要竭尽全力地执行合同。因此，如果延误的部分责任是由他的错误引起，那么，根据情况，其错误可以解释为他不够努力。

业主为工程进展所提出的任何合理要求，承包商都必须照办。业主要求承包商挽回延误时间，支付额外费用而不给予补偿，是不合理的。但合同上附有这样的条款，就工程进度而言，承包人明确的责任就是服从业主的指挥。

这两项责任是紧密相联的。如果业主要求并授权采取措施加快进度而且还给以适当的报酬，那么承包商就有责任去实施。

这里为工程延期提供两套可选择的办法——选择 1 和选择 2。延期的理由不同（选择 2 理由更宽）但是承包商的职责都一样，承包商的职责见流程图 12-1。合同明确规定了承包商必须遵守的各项细则：

一旦承包商认为工程受到延误或工程将有可能要延误，因而工程不能按期交付时，他必须立即书面通知业主。通知必须具体详细，现场会议记录是不够的。

通知必须详细说明情况并对他认为有权延长的时间给予充分且详细的说明，通知内容必须尽可能的充分明了。

承包商必须提供业主所需要的进一步情况，使业主能够更好履行责任，从而估算出一个公正合理的延长期。

一般情况下，承包商没有义务通知延误的情况，只有在他希望得到一个延长期时，才须发出通知。

然而，承包商应当注意，他若未能及时发出通知，业主就可以推迟同意延期，直到最终证书签发之前才给他延期许可。因此承包商适时地认真地履行所有职责完全是为了他自己的利益。

第13单元

平面图形状

建筑物的形状对其工程造价有很大影响。一般说来，建筑物形状越简单，造价就越低。随着建筑物的长度延长或变窄，或者轮廓变得更加复杂或不规则，周长与楼面面积的比也会增加，造价也随之增多。有关周长与楼面面积关系的重要性将在本单元中做更详尽的探讨。不规则的轮廓也会因为其它原因而导致造价增高：放样、施工及管道铺设都很可能变得更加复杂而使其费用更高。需要增加的费用远不止于此，砌砖和屋面工程也因其整个工程更加复杂而会更加耗费资金。建筑物外形的稍许改动便可能引起造价的增大。建筑师和业主了解这一点是很重要的。

虽然最简单的平面形状（即正方形建筑物）建起来最省钱，但未必总是可行。在寓所，小办公室，学校和医院等地方，人们更注重在建筑物的大部分地方能得到充足的自然光线。在一个大型的方形建筑里面，中心部位经常采光不足，而且，设计和内部设施的布局也会遇到很多麻烦。因此，虽然矩形建筑比等面积的正方形建筑造价要高（因后者的周长与楼面面积之比较小），但是，从实用或功能方面以及从美学角度考虑，人们可能会选择矩形方案。

某些种类的建筑因其本身的特征反过来决定了其造型形式和形状。以旅馆为例，从视觉方面考虑，为了给旅客提供良好的观赏环境，为了突出地平线上耸立的高楼的广告效果，旅馆要建得高些。其形状和楼面面积与每层中最经济合算的住房间数有着密不可分的关系，而最经济合算的住房数一般在40到50之间。这就决定了楼房应建成高耸的厚板状而不是塔形。细高的塔状建筑从美学角度来看是很理想的，但其可用面积与楼面的总建筑面积之比相对较小，而致使造价高得让人望而生畏。

有时候，建筑地点本身也会决定建筑物的型式或形状。在某些情况下，设计人员感到有必要劝说业主在周围可买到地皮的情况下再买一些土地，以使该项目更经济一些。浪费一部分畸形场地以确保建成一个形状规则而又经济的建筑是值得的。若是建一座高度约为

8到10层的条状结构建筑物,仅是消防方面的考虑就可能决定了楼房的最佳长度,以确保净面积与建筑面积之比最大。

建筑物的外形也会受到将来使用方式的影响。例如:建筑厂房时,决定因素可能会是制造过程间的相互协调以及各种机器与成品的形状。而学校、住所、医院以及在某种程度上还包括办公楼,其形状在很大程度上受到采光的制约。要想让建筑物内的多数房间白天由自然光线照明,建筑物的进深就会受到限制,要么就必须安装高大的窗户,以弥补建筑物增加了的进深,但这样一来就会增加楼层高度。在这种情况下,其宗旨就是找到一个理想的折衷解决方案。这一方案既能把照明因素又能把建筑造价考虑进去。进深较大的房间会导致周长与楼面面积之比减少,从而使得建筑、维修和采暖费用降低。但是,省下来的钱可能会被增大的照明费用所抵消。较高房间的情况与此恰恰相反。如果需要设置房间多,可把外墙作为房间的墙壁,这样可以省去不这样做时所需的房间之间的隔墙数量。因此,有时可以增加建筑物的长度,以便可以从脊柱状的走廊的任何一边进入房间,而建筑物不必造得进深大,且带有复杂的供出入房间用的走廊网,也不必为里面的房间提供可能需要的人工通风设备。

第14单元

投资者的目的

投资过程的第一步就是要弄清投资者的目的、目标以及各种限制因素。若不进行这一步,那么投资的可行性就无法确定。除了价格上涨、减税带来的各种好处和金融杠杆作用这些显而易见的因素外,我们还探讨一下个人或公司投资房地产的一些更为明确的理由。一些投资者之所以寻求实实在在的房地产拥有权,是因为他们感到房地产比其它金融资产更安全、更有价值、更容易看得见摸得着。在持有房地产期间能获得相当收入的机会对于许多寻求现款收益的人来说具有吸引力。房地产较低的定金支付要求,有了房地产,就能够贷到款,以及在投资者决定出手时对地产增值的期望等都更进一步加强了这份吸引力。更大的回收价值(将来出手的价格)也一直诱惑着投资者,尤其是考虑到时下延期支付税款的各种好处和最近关于降低资金收益税率的税法变更的情况时更是如此。

最后,通过定期支付分期偿还债务的办法,投资者可以经过一段时间的财产价值积累而增强其财产拥有权。虽然这一积累较为缓慢,但是假若房地产值不下降,那么在一段时间内偿还本金也会使拥有者的财产价值有所增加。这样既会补充经过一段时间而增长的房地产价值,又会使财产价值进一步增长。

对于投资者来说,什么才是合适的目标或目的呢?许多投资者希望在投资财产持有期间能获取最多的收入、利润、现金流转或减税带来的好处。另一些人则愿意放弃这些利益而希望在出手时趁财产增值大赚一笔。有的试图运用各种收益率衡量法来衡量这种收益成果;而另一些人则通过衡量他们个人财产增加量或他们净资产(或财富)状况来估算收益情况。不过,每一位投资者最理想的目的都是取决于自身的目标,对风险的承受力,以及个人的兴趣和爱好。对许多投资者来说,这一目标就是能最大限度地获取财富或净资产。

投资是什么?

较早的投资分析把投资和投机区分开来。投机常与为挣大钱而担大风险或与无担保的冒险有关,这些投机者常借他人之资本为自己谋利益;而投资则被看作是一种常有稳定收入而并不用借贷资金的有保证的财产获取。

令人惊奇的是,这些区分法的许多部分如今仍被采用。不过,把投机与投资区分开来也并非易事。如果一个人为赚得一大笔收益而对购置房地产产生兴趣,并且尽其所能地对某一区域的房地产加以分析研究,那么我们能把他看成是投机者而不是投资者吗?或者说,如果投资者对财产的期望持有期很短,或者由于社区的发展,增值期望率较高,或者投资者相信此类房地产的期望增值率会较高,那么,这个所谓的投机者与其它的投资者有没有什么不同呢?显然,答案是否定的。以往关于投机和投资的划分现已无用了,而且在某些方面是相当含糊不清的。

风险和收益并存

风险和收益是分不开的。收益率高的投资机会常常伴有很大的风险。同样地,那些看来较安全、风险不大的房地产投资将来的收益一般也不大。就我们的市场经济而论,由于市场上的买卖双方都一直在估计日益变化的市场条件对房地产价值所产生的影响,所以必须对风险与收益之间的关系有所考虑。对投资产生极大影响的各种变化因素也会对买卖双方看中的项目预期收益和(或)风险产生类似影响。因此,市场价格的涨落受到变化的预计作用的影响。由于人不能"没有投入就有所回报"(若没有市场上别人不曾掌握的最佳信息),所以,风险和收益是并存的。

在风险和收益并存的市场经济里,人们会期望找到风险与需求收益率之间的平衡关系。由于投资期间资金提前利用,所以不冒风险仍有收益。不过,随着所期望的收益量的增加,风险量也随之增大。在这个分析中,投资者可以随意挑选要承担的风险量,而这些风险则会变成预期收益。

第15单元

合同(概论、确立项目及准备范围)

合同被定义为两方或多方当事人之间所作的承诺,它通过法律来强行实施。因此,为了保护业主和承包商双方的利益,合同是必不可少的。

概论

业主和承包人的目的大不相同。一般说来,前者努力以最低的造价按时竣工,而后者的目的是多赚取利润。这一点为许多业主所忽略。

有几个合同标准条件，它们便于签定双方都能遵守的法律文件。这些合同有的对承包商有利，有的则对业主有利。换句话说。风险的担子由相关的一方承担或双方共同承担。选择最适合其团体及项目需要的合同是符合项目经理的利益的。

有鉴于此，签定合同时必须经常考虑下列诸因素：

1. 工程范围，即工程所涉及的范围或领域。工程施工过程中，工程项目内容的增减会增加或减少相关环节的工作量，而且任何设计上的变动都得仔细推敲，以确定它们是否会影响工程的范围。

2. 时间。范围和时间紧密相连，而且制定决策必须经常考虑时间对于范围增减的影响。如果一个工程的竣工日期很重要，那么要扩大工程的范围就需要加快进度，而与之相关的额外费用必须确定，并且这些费用对于财务方面，即投资收益的影响，也必须估算出来。

3. 价格。价格也与范围和时间紧密相关。在这一单元中，讨论的大部分内容将是关于合同对价格的影响，以及有助于保持价格稳定的各种鼓励及惩罚条款。

签定合同前要采取八个基本步骤，这些都已表示在图 15-1 中。下面将依次讨论头四个步骤。

确立项目

确立项目是导致合同签定的一系列活动的第一步。这里所作的决定将会对整个合同前期步骤以及管理阶段产生影响。

项目确定必须与团体的总目标紧密结合。常有这种情况，一个项目被选定，而且工作做了很长一段时间，却发现该项目同公司的总体计划相冲突。

例如：营销部门可能会预测到生产能力有计划的发展会带来一个光明的未来销售前景。然而进一步考虑后会发现，新旧计划接轨所产生的工程方面的问题使得整个工程不合算。若采取付给股东较高的股息、对发展投入较少资金的内部政策，那么工程的进展则可能受到阻碍。

若准备阶段时间很长，那么确立项目就更为困难，而且影响决策的因素频繁地变化，令人难受。70 年代中期，对中央电业局所面临的窘境有过大量的报导。当时，他们 60 年代作出的发展计划没有实现。结果是根据前 10 年的决定建造了大量令人尴尬的、闲置的发电站。

准备范围

范围或者说工程所涉及的方面，前面已经简要提到。这一阶段包括实际工作的实施、进度安排、材料提供、场地要求及工程标准的采用等方面。

项目一旦确定，就得开始设计工作，以确定工程的准确性。项目经理要决定是自行设计还是设计与施工总包。通常，如果项目独特，那么就该采用前一个方案。如果该

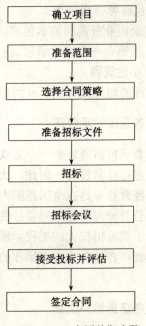

图 15-1 合同前期步骤

团体不具有这方面的能力，那么就要请顾问。

在此阶段，项目经理的压力最大，因为他不仅要运用自己的技术才能，而且还要协调所有设计中出现的信息、资料和数据，以确保各项建议经济上不超支，安全上有保障。顾问人员对一幢工业综合楼的建筑装饰的设计可能包括建造一些施工起来困难而又很不经济的角、斜面或曲线等。尽管这些建议使建筑物看上去更美观，但是它们对最终造价的巨大影响足以使人们有必要对整个计划重新考虑。

必须制定一个有明确竣工日期的方案。如果竣工日期的推迟致使收入总额受到损失，那么损失部分应按时间和开支进行估算。如果不牵涉收益，比如道路建筑，那么应计算出延期的"时机代价"。同样，也应了解提前竣工带来的好处，以便把激励因素记入合同里。

第 16 单元

承包商与分包商的关系（I）

引言

总承包商与分包商之间的关系是人与人的关系。本文旨在对双方所碰到的一些问题做一评述，并试图解答这些问题，以期对建筑队伍的所有成员有所裨益。

总承包商的分类

承包商可分为三类：
1. 全国业务范围的承包商；
2. 城镇业务范围的承包商；
3. 小建筑商。

这样的划分没有把所有的建筑商都包括进去，其目的只是为了便于本文的讨论。

全国业务范围的承包商

此类承包商通常是一个公众有限责任公司，它对其股东负责，并由精通专业或懂技术的经理进行经营管理。因此，比起小承包商来，此类承包商与分包商的关系要疏远一些。

其经营业务是在全国范围内，所以它与大型的、全国业务范围的分包商的关系更为密切。一旦与分包商建立起良好关系，那么要变更就会遇到强大的阻力。

由于能承担较大的工程，所以此类承包商可能不会象其它承包商那样面临着强烈的竞争。因此，在从事这方面运作的专家参与下，这类承包商有可能通过谈判得到较优越的条件。

城镇业务范围的承包商

此类公司的业务范围有一定的限制，因此，要更加充分地发挥当地分包商的作用。此类公司往往是家族式企业，尽管利润也是其追求的目标，但它对产品的质量也往往看得很重。因为他们承建的每一幢建筑物都将成为公司的一座纪念碑。他们建成什么样的楼房，大家有目共睹。由于经理或业主要参与预算、合同管理、检验或工地管理，所以，公司的经营状况与他们有着直接的利害关系。

小建筑商

小建筑商往往在有限的地域内开展业务。其负责人时常在工地工作，因此，一般说来，他的实践经验要比其专业知识丰富。小建筑商通常是不错的手艺人，干的活儿常使业主感到称心如意。小建筑商一般与在同一契约基础上经营的小分包商打交道。

分包商的分类

分包商的主要类型的划分及其主要业务范围可参见附录。他们可分为：
1. 专家分包商；
2. 行业分包商；
3. 专供劳务的分包商。

专家分包商

专家分包商提供设计方案和专门的服务，他通常是被指定的。在有限竞争的情况下，他为工程开价。由于其工作的重复性，所以工作具有效率。此类分包商认为有必要组织一个经营机构，并由其技术代理定期访问建筑师和承包商。

为了便于建筑师从多个专家分包商中进行挑选，分包商可能在准备报价单的同时，还得准备一份设计方案。这就意味着要支出一笔额外的费用，而这种费用必须在公司的一般管理费中反映出来。

行业分包商

行业分包商总是由总承包商选定，但是合同常常规定建筑师必须同意这种选择。行业分包商与建造商关系密切，经常接触。他将传统的工种一概揽下，但很少需要销售方面的专门知识，因为他过去的经历为他积累了销售方面的经验。一般说来，他们不提供设计方案，只提供劳务、材料和监督管理。因此，他们的一般管理费用要少于专家分包商。

专供劳务的分包商

近年来发生了很大的变化，由从前的直接雇用技工变成雇用专供劳务的分包商。有些合同，尤其是象住宅这样重复性的项目，整个合同全由分包商雇用的劳力承包下来已司空见惯。

由于越来越多地雇用专供劳务的分包商，就有了对此类分包商的纳税进行管理的法规，即714号证书。总承包商必须弄清楚分包商是否具有国家税务局颁发的有效证书。如若没有，总承包商就必须从分包商的酬金中扣除30％的劳务费。

因此，许多这样的分包商都按照有关规定组成了公司。他们为建筑业提供有价值的服务，并由于其一般管理费用较低而成为提供直接劳力极有竞争力的候选对象。

Appendix III   Key to Exercises

UNIT ONE
Reading Comprehension
  I . 1. C 2. D 3. A 4. D 5. A
  II . 1. b 2. e 3. a 4. d 5. b

Vocabulary
  I . 1. accumulated 2. was disrupted 3. mortgage
    4. strife 5. to go around
  II . 1. c 2. e 3. a 4. d 5. b

UNIT TWO
Reading Comprehension
  I . 1. B 2. A 3. D 4. A 5. C
  II . 1. d 2. a 3. e 4. b 5. c

Vocabulary
  I . 1. arduous 2. manufactured 3. interacted
    4. maintenance 5. endure
  II . 1. e 2. d 3. b 4. a 5. c

UNIT THREE
Reading Comprehension
  I . 1. A 2. D 3. D 4. D 5. D
  II . 1. b 2. d 3. c 4. e 5. a

Vocabulary
  I . 1. facilitated 2. necessitate 3. extract
    4. simplify 5. assess
  II . 1. c 2. e 3. a 4. d 5. b

UNIT FOUR
Reading Comprehension
  I . 1. D 2. C 3. B 4. B 5. C
  II . 1. b 2. e 3. d 4. a 5. c

Vocabulary
    I. 1. anticipate   2. guarantee   3. indicative
        4. limitation   5. caption
    II. 1. d   2. b   3. e   4. a   5. c

UNIT FIVE
Reading Comprehension
    I. 1. B   2. C   3. A   4. D   5. C
    II. 1. T   2. F   3. T   4. F   5. F

Vocabulary
    I. 1. bidding   2. prospective   3. reimbursable
        4. modifications   5. designated
    II. 1. c   2. e   3. a   4. b   5. d

UNIT SIX
Reading Comprehension
    I. 1. A   2. C   3. B   4. B   5. D
    II. 1. F   2. T   3. F   4. F   5. T

Vocabulary
    I. 1. lease   2. minimal   3. premises
        4. superfluous   5. finance
    II. 1. d   2. e   3. b   4. c   5. a

UNIT SEVEN
Reading Comprehension
    I. 1. D   2. D   3. D   4. B   5. C
    II. 1. F   2. F   3. T   4. F   5. T

Vocabulary
    I. 1. guarantee   2. Inadequate   3. compensation
        4. defined   5. essence
    II. 1. b   2. e   3. c   4. a   5. d

UNIT EIGHT
Reading Comprehension

Ⅰ.1.C   2.B   3.C   4.D   5.C
Ⅱ.1.F   2.T   3.F   4.F   5.T

Vocabulary
Ⅰ. 1. acquisition   2. unambiguous   3. defective
   4. minimized   5. formulates
Ⅱ. 1. c   2. e   3. d   4. a   5. b

UNIT NINE
Reading Comprehension
Ⅰ.1.D   2.A   3.D   4.C   5.C
Ⅱ.1.T   2.T   3.F   4.F   5.F

Vocabulary
Ⅰ.1.d   2.e   3.a   4.c   5.b
Ⅱ. 1. envisaged   2. implementation   3. depreciation
   4. fluctuation   5. rehabilitation

UNIT TEN
Reading Comprehension
Ⅰ.1.B   2.D   3.C   4.D   5.A
Ⅱ.1.T   2.F   3.T   4.F   5.T

Vocabulary
Ⅰ.1.d   2.c   3.b   4.e   5.a
Ⅱ. 1. potential   2. accelerate   3. phase
   4. commence   5. inflationary

UNIT ELEVEN
Reading Comprehension
Ⅰ.1.D   2.C   3.B   4.A   5.D
Ⅱ.1.F   2.T   3.T   4.T   5.F

Vocabulary
Ⅰ.1.b   2.d   3.e   4.a   5.c
Ⅱ. 1. comparable   2. periodic   3. accounting
   4. enterprise   5. subsidizes

UNIT TWELVE
Reading Comprehension
I . 1. A   2. D   3. C   4. C   5. B
II . 1. T   2. F   3. T   4. F   5. F

Vocabulary
I . 1. b   2. d   3. a   4. e   5. c
II . 1. provisions   2. notify   3. estimate
4. obligation   5. specify

UNIT THIREEN
Reading Comprehension
I . 1. B   2. D   3. A   4. D   5. C
II . 1. (4)   2. (1)   3. (5)   4. (3)   5. (2)

Vocabulary
I . 1. unit cost   2. ratio   3. layout
4. offset   5. storey
II . 1. e   2. d   3. b   4. a   5. c

UNIT FOURTEEN
Reading Comprehension
I . 1. C   2. A   3. C   4. B   5. D
II . 1. accumulation of property value as a result of satisfying mortgage over time
2. selling prices in the future
3. balance between opposing forces
4. a part of the full price paid at the time of buying something, with the rest to be paid later
5. property in the form of land and houses

Vocabulary
I . 1. risks   2. leverage   3. purchased
4. assets   5. return
II . 1. C   2. A   3. C   4. C   5. B

UNIT FIFTEEN
Reading Comprehension
I . 1. C   2. D   3. D   4. D   5. B

II. 1. e   2. g   3. a   4. c   5. b

Vocabulary
I . 1. phase   2: ploughing back   3. tender
    4. penalty   5. marketing
II. 1. revenues   2. dividends   3. incentives
    4. defer   5. placed

UNIT SIXTEEN

Reading Comprehension
I . 1. D   2. A   3. B   4. B   5. A
II. 1. T   2. F   3. F   4. T   5. F

Vocabulary
I . 1. operatives   2. certificates   3. conditions
    4. building team   5. satisfied
II. 1. liability   2. quotation   3. payment
    4. deducted   5. representative

图书在版编目（CIP）数据

建筑类专业英语. 建筑管理与财会. 第1册/陆铁镛，孙玮主编. —北京：中国建筑工业出版社，1997(2005重印)
高等学校试用教材
ISBN 978-7-112-03038-5

Ⅰ. 建... Ⅱ. ①陆... ②孙... Ⅲ. ①建筑学-英语-高等学校-教材②建筑企业-财务管理-英语-高等学校-教材 Ⅳ. H31

中国版本图书馆 CIP 数据核字（2005）第 106700 号

本书系按国家教委颁布的《大学英语专业阅读阶段教学基本要求》组织编写的专业英语教材。本册包括宏观经济学、建筑经济、会计、管理会计师在决策中的作用、现金预测、承包、投资、合同、质量保证等方面内容。全书安排16个单元，每单元除正课文外，还有两篇阅读材料，均配有必要的注释。正课文还配有词汇表和练习，书后附有总词汇表、参考译文和练习答案。供本专业学生使用。

高等学校试用教材
建 筑 类 专 业 英 语
建筑管理与财会
第一册

陆铁镛 孙 玮 　　　主编
文育玲 李 红 吴来安　　
黄 莉 唐之远 彭志军　　编
任 宏 　　　主审

*

中国建筑工业出版社出版、发行（北京西郊百万庄）
各地新华书店、建筑书店经销
北京建筑工业印刷厂印刷

*

开本：787×1092毫米 1/16 印张：12 字数：287千字
1997年6月第一版　2008年6月第七次印刷
印数：8601—9800册　定价：17.00元
ISBN 978-7-112-03038-5
(14976)

版权所有　翻印必究
如有印装质量问题，可寄本社退换
（邮政编码 100037）